STRIKE YOUR BALANCE

HOW TO BE AT PEACE WITH YOURSELF

SRIHARI PALANGALA

STARDOM BOOKS

STARDOM BOOKS

WORLDWIDE

www.StardomBooks.com

STARDOM BOOKS

A Division of Stardom Publishing

and infoYOGIS Technologies.

105-501 Silverside Road

Wilmington, DE 19809

FIRST EDITION SEPTEMBER 2021

Stardom Books

STRIKE YOUR BALANCE
/HOW TO BE AT PEACE WITH YOURSELF

Srihari Palangala

p. 136
cm. 13.5 X 21.5

Category: Self-help/Self-Management/General

ISBN-13: 978-1-7369486-5-1

DEDICATION

I would like to dedicate this book to my readers, the seekers of balance and inner peace. Even as the world changes rapidly in our personal and professional spheres, your efforts to surf these waves in the pursuit of a successful career whilst leading a wholesome and eventful life is nothing short of remarkable.

I hope, my dear readers, that you recognize the tensions we identify in this book. I sincerely wish my book helps you negotiate these tensions and find your balance in life.

CONTENTS

ACKNOWLEDGMENTS

To my wife for encouraging me to write this book. Our
conversations and actions on leading a balanced life, be it in the
professional or personal domain have guided our life.
To our son for whom I write this book so that he can incorporate
these perspectives in his life.
To my parents, sisters and family who have always trusted me in
full faith on the choices made.

"I have been an ardent student of work-life balance and what it means to me in today's world. Srihari's words gave meaning to my learning, my understanding and my emotions. Simple yet powerful in its expression!"

Ankur Warikoo
Founder@nearbuy.com

I loved your introduction; I was intrigued to continue with the reading as you started with the more familiar iPhone, moving on to android, the age of technology leading to e-shopping, PayPal, Paytm and Google pay. This got me thinking about where this thought process was leading to and getting the clear message you seem to be arriving at, quoting you, "world demands you to keep up with the pace".

"Losing the training wheel" is one of the chapters I loved; so beautifully analysed. Your analogy is so apt, comparing the learning of riding a bicycle to our lives and how we are forced to pick up our confidence when we slowly lose support yet continue on the path to success. I am also amazed at your quotes from Swami Vivekananda, Robert Frost, and excerpts from Gita, which is so apt to the situation.

I strongly stand by your statement anger surfaces when we detect a deficiency in ourselves.

You have so beautifully and subtly described small incidences to put forth the consequences of our accountability, ability, attitude, experience, behaviour, and judgement.

You rightly stated that today's younger generation's challenges are far more complex than what we have all faced.

It was a wonderful journey of thoughts that you took me through. Each of the chapters had its own unique takeaways.

Ms. Shantha Chandran
Principal, National Public School

This easy-to-read book packs in a huge number of practical and useful tips on maintaining inner balance while facing the challenges of many contradictions emerging these days in professional and personal life. Srihari's insights drawn from his own experience on managing his corporate career and personal life effectively, embracing change, and balancing home and work are particularly valuable.

Dr S. Raghunath
Professor of Strategy
Chairman South Asia Board Academy of International Business
Indian Institute of Management Bangalore

PART A: INTRODUCTION

1
LOSING THE TRAINING WHEELS

There used to be a time when the fastest way you could get a message was through a telegram. Now that word has come to be associated with an instant messaging service.

The first *iPhone* came in the year 2007, and the first *Android* phone was released in 2008. Today, we see hundreds of different variations in smartphones and millions of different features embedded into them. The fact that this sort of revolutionary change escalated so rapidly justifies that the world we know is changing, and it is changing at a pace never witnessed before.

This change is multi-faceted; the many innovations in technology drive it. Blockchain, quantum computing, AI and IoT are no longer subjects of science fiction but a part of our everyday lives. Over a century ago, *Ford* revolutionized work culture when it introduced the assembly line production. Ford standardized work that led to reliable products at lower costs.

However, this is the age of digital technology. The assembly line had mechanized work; technology and the internet have added data to the mix. The challenges we face today are far more complex than what our predecessors faced. Previously a marketing campaign would have revolved around clear signals involving clever slogans or eye-catching promotional campaigns.

Today, marketing can be individualized based on consumer interests that may be analyzed through social media interactions and internet shopping. The internet has also reduced the need for a central base of communications. Applications like *Slack* and *Zoom*, among others, have made communication easier and decentralized. With the addition of data to mechanics, work is now more focused on problems rather than function.

Even if people specialize in any function, they are hired to solve potential problems. An employee or a team are now expected to work across lines on multiple projects and contribute if and when required. One may be expected to complete different projects and fill in at different functions within those projects.

Rapid advances in technology, transportation, global finances and communication have seen the world enter into a race where you need to better your game constantly. The advent of globalization has also witnessed the rise of hyper-competition. Just look at the data wars of India. You had companies suddenly adjusting their mobile data charges based on the low prices set by *Jio* when it made its entry into the market.

Then there is the arrival of the e-commerce sites. Thanks to this, activities like shopping can now be conducted with a few clicks. There are new mobile phones released into the market with their own strategic advantages, every two months. You might have noticed the repeated usage of terms like budget flagship models or budget flagship killer models to describe phones and their specifications.

Even the food market has now been turned into a hypercompetitive digital venue with apps like *Zomato* and *Swiggy* in India; these come with their own set of attractive discounts. On a broader scale, there are ride-faring apps like *Uber* and *Lyft*. Once *Apple* introduced the world's first *iPhone*, the term smartphone put forth by *Blackberry* was redefined.

Soon, *Samsung* joined in, and the phone market changed worldwide. Within the same market, we have also seen the rise and fall of mobile phone makers like *HTC*.

Today, the global markets have been inundated by mobile phone makers who've brought forth phones at budget prices with high specifications. Someone is always setting the bar, and others always respond.

Tesla, which produces electric vehicles mainly in the sedan market, decided to bring out an all-electric pickup truck called the *Cybertruck*. This resulted in leading pickup truck manufacturers like *Ford*, *GMC*, and even other electric vehicle manufacturers like *Rivian* announcing all-electric pickup trucks of their own. Space, too, has not been seen as the last frontier. Once seen as a domain which only countries with big pockets could explore, Elon Musk breached it with *Space X*. However, now we may be on the cusp of commercial space travel with *Virgin Atlantic* and *Blue Origin* making their successful maiden flights in 2021. Both Branson and Bezos may have fired the first shot, but as per one UBS report[1], commercial space travel is expected to reach $3 billion by 2030. Moving on, the advent of social media changed everything we knew about communication.

Applications like *WhatsApp*, *Twitter*, *Instagram* and *Facebook* have streamlined the entire process. We also have numerous news channels catering to different genres and languages. You are bound to receive inputs even from video sharing websites like *YouTube*. It is easier to make your voice heard among like-minded people in this digital world, whom you couldn't have reached earlier.

As I mentioned previously, shopping has now become an e-commerce activity. Your purchases and wish lists help the e-commerce sites tailor their adverts to your likes and dislikes. Even your social media likes and interactions are factored in when companies look to market their products to you. Data has become the driving force of the world economy today. Data has also crept into how we make payments. Cheques were once considered sacred, and then your worth was seen in the colour of your credit card.

---

[1] https://www.cnbc.com/2019/03/18/ubs-space-travel-and-space-tourism-a-23-billion-business-in-a-decade.html

Now, even at the most local level, transactions seem to be done with a tap on a mobile phone. Financial transactions that needed days to complete are now done within seconds. When banks with their brick-and-mortar infrastructure couldn't keep up with the pace of technology, entrepreneurs responded with applications like *PayPal, Paytm,* and *Google Pay.* When the financial markets crashed, decentralized currencies like *Bitcoin* and *Ethereum* became the alternative.

Changes can also be seen in our work environments. Even in a field like academia, work has become hypercompetitive. Researchers are always in a rush to publish more papers to drive more funding to their programs. Academic departments know that funding is limited; hence they have to distinguish themselves from the volume of research done. Similarly, any other work or job is bound in such competition. You will find certain people who will constantly push the bar, and you will have to respond. It could be a co-worker, a boss or even a subordinate. You will constantly face these challenges to stay alert, and these challenges are also temporally bound.

Modern technology may have narrowed geographical distances, but it has also made time an important work element. Douglas Adams may have joked about deadlines by saying, *"I love deadlines. I love the whooshing noise they make as they go by."* But deadlines are a crucial part of today's work culture. If you let them whoosh you by, it will come at great personal and organizational costs. As the world has taken up a relentless pace, you are always expected to be on your toes and be punctual. This is why any project undertaken includes deadline management as a critical part of its initial planning and is constantly monitored. Thus, if you were to examine our world today, as seen in the image on the next page, you will find yourself between three elements. This is a world which demands you to keep up with its pace. You are constantly stuck in a race with others who continuously push the bar, and you are expected to respond. Your life could perhaps be seen as a response to these various stimuli. You may also find your interests quantified and find alluring campaigns tailored to your personal likes.

```
        ( Hyper
          competitive
          world )

    ↗                    ↘

( Speed and        ←        ( External
   pace )                      signals )
```

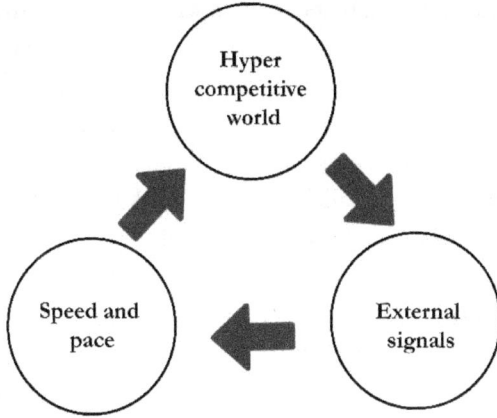

All these challenges come with their own unique set of tensions, and you will find that most of these tensions are interconnected due to the overlays within these three elements.

If you look at our individual lives, our way of life has changed over the last two to three decades. The pandemic has only furthered this stark contrast. Schools went from physical buildings to a laptop and a webcam. If you did not have the latter, you would have to find a way to source them. Our work culture, as noted earlier, has also undergone a fundamental change. The idea of a secure and routine job has become a relic of a bygone era. Instead, it now seems like a "series of projects."

The world today is fast-paced and hyper-connected. Information about anything is available at our fingertips. You could be an engineer and learn to write. You could be a doctor who can learn to code. The beauty of today's world is that it permits intersectionality. There are endless possibilities for you to choose from and refine your individuality. There are far more opportunities and avenues available to the working man/woman today. Numerous jobs are being created every day, and while that sounds great, they also inevitably come with competition. Everyone in today's world is focused on upskilling.

Whether or not you have a secure job, you cannot risk remaining stagnant with your capabilities. There will always be someone who is going to try to replace you. The world is not so forgiving anymore. You rarely get a second chance. It would seem like you have been thrown in at the deep end. There is no guidance and no support. You are expected to keep to the relentless pace.

If I were to offer an analogy, I would ask you to remember how you learnt to ride a bicycle. When you first seated yourself on a cycle, the world would have seemed to go faster. If you rode around your house, you would have found some degree of freedom. However, the moment you wheeled yourself onto the motorway, you would have found that you don't have the same freedom. You are expected to stay on one side of the road. Even when you stick to one side of the road, you would have to stick to a lane. Footpaths were reserved for pedestrians. Even the world around you would seem relentless in its pace.

The vehicles would be faster, and the noise could also deafen you. You would then realise that there are certain signals or indicators to learn when you want to cross to another lane or take a turn. There would be many things to know, and it may seem overwhelming on your first ride on the road.

Of course, you would first ride it with the training wheels—learning to balance. You will also notice people being kind towards you when you have those training wheels attached to your cycle. The training wheels would indicate that you are still learning. However, they may not be as kind when you ride your bicycle without your training wheels. You will find the road even more challenging. The world today, just like the road, seems chaotic and hectic. It constantly demands you to keep up with the pace of its change. It's either keep up or get left behind.

As Swami Vivekananda said, *"Live in the midst of the battle of life. Anyone can keep calm in a cave or when asleep. Stand in the whirl and madness of action and reach the center. If you have found the center, you cannot be moved."* This is the new age maxim of the 'survival of the fittest.' It is in such an age that you have to grow and thrive.

But this brings us to the question, "How do you thrive in such a world?" The first step is to identify the world around you and how it affects you. When you decide to be inquisitive about this world, you will notice that your relations with the world are fraught with contradictions and conflicts. You have to constantly negotiate with these tensions to find a solution to every challenge. Do you remember your first few rides on a bicycle? How well do you remember those experiences? You may remember some of the sights seen or the small races won against some of your peers. You may remember the scenic routes and the memories associated with them. How many of you remember the falls?

Unless it was a significant accident, you might not remember many. But there will be one indelible memory: The first time you lost the training wheels. Your parent or guardian would have been there beside you. They would have been holding the seat behind you and assuring you never to let go. Thanks to this assurance, you would slowly loosen yourself and enjoy the ride. Suddenly you would feel as if you were flying. Little did you know that the grounding force (your guardian's support) had already been withdrawn, and you were all on your own. If you were an adventurous kid, you would have taken off with rapture. Sooner or later, you would have stopped or fallen due to the foreign nature of keeping your balance and pedaling simultaneously.

However, if you were more of a circumspect kid, you would have stopped immediately and looked back at your guardian in remonstration. Of all the rides you would have done, that one should be the most vivid. What you would eventually remember subconsciously is how you learned to balance yourself on a two-wheeled ride. This muscle memory would play a leading role when you moved onto other two-wheeled rides like motorcycles and scooters.

Try and recollect that feeling. Apply it to where you are right now. You will find that your parents or the world at large are no longer holding you to help balance in this dynamic world. You are now riding your cycle without the training wheels.

They have let go so that you can move unassisted. Even your highly vaunted college degree, you will find, is just an entry ticket to a rollercoaster ride. There is no guaranteed success.

And yet, you will find yourself trying your best for it, often even experiencing the joys of it. The word 'success' will evolve with you. You will find yourself seeing it in a different light at every phase of your life.

Although colleges and workplaces may equip you with the tools to deal with the nuances of life, it is up to you to find the right tool and finetune the adjustments required. You must learn to define life in your own way. Remember, we may be inspired by people around us and motivated by different causes, but the life we live is like nobody else's. What might have seemed like a road full of chaos initially will eventually open up into a pathway full of opportunities.

Dealing with contradictions and choices

Let's consider this situation. Say you are working towards a promotion. This pursuit would have you overwork and miss out on quality family time. The work may also have you travel a lot more and for longer durations. Such a work schedule is bound to bring forth tensions within a family. It could be especially troubling if you are a newlywed or a new parent. What do you do now? Will you work harder to ensure your promotion or cut back and desire more family time?

Let's consider another example. Say you are a reticent person. However, you cannot spend your life alone. Human beings are social creatures, and we look for companionship to tide over troubled times and share joy during happier occasions. However, as an introvert, you may find socializing activities bothersome. But you may also be worried about people considering you as standoffish if you keep rejecting such opportunities. This fear could result in you accepting too many invitations when it may not even benefit you. What will you do if you were in this situation? The two examples given are some of the contradictions that we face in our daily lives.

8

In other words, they are two seemingly diametrically opposing situations, and neither of them is an entirely correct way to live your life. They present a conundrum. Let us take the first example of wanting to fast-track your career. This choice could mean that you compromise on vibrant and quality familial relationships or a rich social life. How about diets? Would you want to eat the things you love, even if it comes at the cost of healthy living?

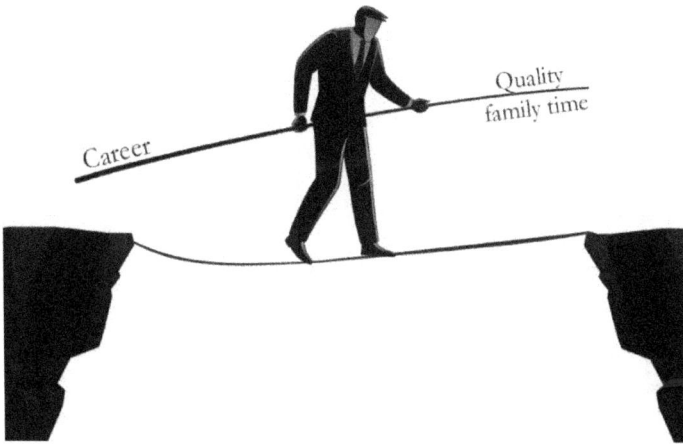

Balancing career and family is like a tightrope act

If you were to think about it, life is a multitude of choices. We could stress the importance of private life and personal space, yet rush to upload the latest photos onto *Facebook* and *Instagram* with the trendiest hashtags.

There could be scientists who pray to God and priests who preach even when they have lost faith. Each choice seems to pull us in many directions simultaneously. There are always a set of tensions involved and are at play.

If you were to examine all the choices, you would realize that there is no absolute answer to these choices. You figure out what works for you, and you live accordingly. For instance, if you were to opt for a healthy diet, you figure out a way to add in a cheat meal or two to satisfy your cravings. There is no right or correct answer.

You figure out what works for you, and you make peace with that decision. The only exception is when it comes to your values and the law of the land. There is no negotiation when it comes to the rules of the land. Always adhere to the highest standards in clear black-and-white situations.

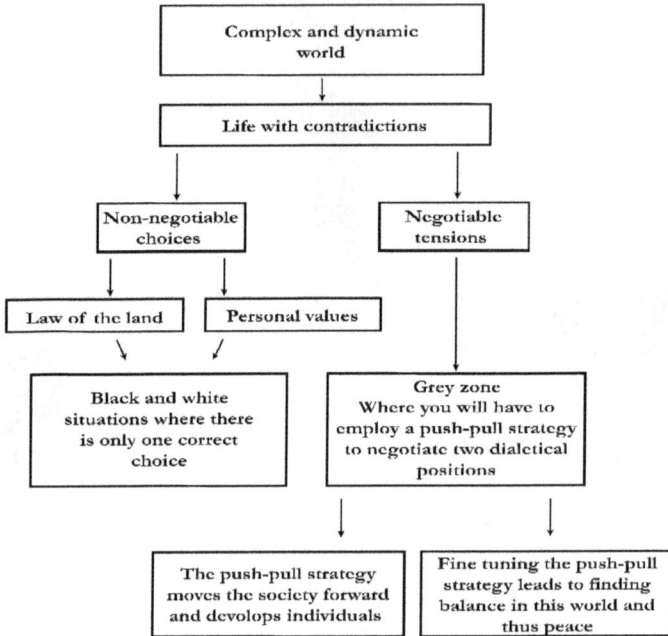

But in other areas, you will find a lot of grey zones. You have to negotiate with these contrasting positions and have to work out the best option for you.

However, you will soon realize that this balancing act is never static. When you are faced with similar tensions later, you will learn that the same choice may not work anymore. The world has become dynamic, and you have to respond appropriately to the many contradictions you may face. However, do not be flustered by my usage of the word 'contradictions.'

Contradiction, in its very name, comes with a context that seems bad. However, I'll instead contend that it is inherently good. You learn and grow from contradictions. When you participate in contradictions, it is a sign of thought and progress. Even when it comes to intellectual thought, you only grow when you contradict beliefs. If you only indulge in ideas that you think are correct without subjecting them to the fiercest examination from contrasting thoughts, you will be stuck in an echo chamber where you will only hear the same unchallenged perspectives. When you get stuck in this rut, you will be stuck in a regressive intellectual thought process.

Whenever there is movement and action, it can be traced to a contradiction. Positive movement occurs only due to differences. As Swami Vivekananda wrote, motion is possible in this world only due to lost balance. If you were to think about it, some of the greatest literature, art, science, and philosophy happened only because someone investigated the contradictions. Avant-garde art can be traced to the protest against war and cultural and intellectual conformity.

Philosophical thoughts and theories are essentially contradictory responses to other thoughts and theories. SD Savransky, in a study[2], looked at inventive problems and defined them as a problem that includes a contradiction for which a solution is not found. Newton discovered gravity when an apple fell down, and he found a contradiction when the other apples stayed on the branches of a tree. When we delve into the differences generated by contradictions, we nourish a creative spirit.

This creative spirit is born because we as humans can compartmentalize. We can classify our emotions, practices, and knowledge. Let us consider the act of committing falsehood. We know that lying is a bad habit. However, sometimes, your one lie could end up saving a person's life. This act of falsehood isn't bound by the same context.

---

[2] https://www.aaai.org/Papers/Symposia/Spring/1999/SS-99-07/SS99-07-020.pdf

So, we can compartmentalize the act of lying according to the context we find ourselves in. That said, compartmentalizing is an art you need to fine-tune to navigate the contradictions in your life.

When you break down the contradictions in your life, you will realize that contradictions bring forth perspective and can even inspire you. The problem, however, lies in how we perceive these contradictions. Due to the dialectical nature of contradictions, we think of our choices as being only one over the other.

Here, I could bring upon the adages such as, "too much of anything is a bad thing" or "do not put all your eggs in one basket." I want you to understand that life is not a set of binary choices. It is about navigating these differences and finding your path forward. It is about finding your middle ground and your balance within these dualities. In the following chapters, we will explore some of these dualities and reflect on negotiating them.

Satisfaction comes with inner balance.

So how do we find that balance? If we were to return to the cycling analogy, just like how you felt the counterforces, there are counterforces in your life right now. Just like how we experienced the thrill of cycling in our later rides, we need to learn the art of balancing. Swami Vivekananda says that living in this material world with a sense of balance is the hardest thing to do.

It is vital to have a balance between many conflicting ideas and thoughts - the sense of balance helps keep your mind and heart "in the center." Balance spirituality while living in a material world. Balance a selfish outlook with one that is caring for others. Balance being pushy and urgency with patience.

The list can be quite endless. Never let anything (good or bad) destabilize you for too long! The *Bhagavad Gita* also stresses the importance of maintaining a stable mindset. Some verses extol the virtues of being a *Stithaprajna*. While it may be easy to dismiss it as a form of asceticism or renunciation, it is the philosophy that we should look to adopt.

```
                        ┌──────────▶  With external action
   Maintain             │
inner balance           ┤
                        │
                        └──────────▶  With inner thoughts
```

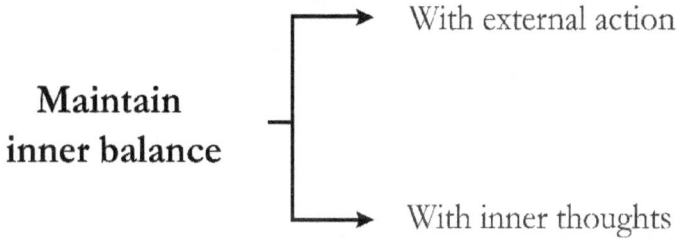

Gita's verse goes, *"He who is regulated in his habits of eating, sleeping, recreation, and work can mitigate all material pains by practicing the yoga system."* [Ch.6.17]

So, what does a balanced life mean? It means that you participate in the world around you but keep your inner bearings, guided by what you believe is right. It is about knowing that the good comes with the bad. You recognize that life has its ebb and flow, and to have balance, you must build a strong sense of discipline around what you will allow yourself to do and what you will not. Balance comes in actions and thoughts.

Your actions (what the external world sees) cannot be at the extreme of any spectrum. And your thoughts (this is far more important, and it is what only you can see) -- need to be balanced as well. Each has a way of influencing the other.

Hence, be balanced in your actions and train your mind to be balanced in your thoughts. Let us return to the earlier example of career vs. family. Where will you find your balance? It is about negotiating the right fit for you. The reactive and limited mindset would be to confuse yourself.

Finding your balance is about weighing your options and finding your way. We shall explore this very contradiction in a later chapter. Balance is about finding the right fit. When you spend the time to strike a balance, you will accept your decisions as you look back in time. You will not repent. How about we examine a situation in the simplest context?

You would have had experienced or heard of others buying something so flashy that it overrode the caution that we didn't need it. It is only after the purchase that we regret giving into that momentary desire. Let us take a more significant example. Let us say you get an opportunity to switch jobs. This switch comes with a great salary package. Would you take the job? In a perfect world, your answer would be a 'yes.'

So how about we add the imperfections? Let us say the new job would mean you work for longer hours. I'm sure that would add a wrinkle to that choice. Additionally, let us say you do not hear good things about your prospective boss. Perhaps the growth opportunities are better at your current job. You cannot weigh all your options and make an appropriate decision when your mind isn't balanced. Only when you are stable in your thoughts can you dissect these issues. So, after careful study, you will not look back with a shadow in your heart when you make a decision. The next time you come across these lines by Robert Frost, you would do so with a sigh of relief and acceptance:

> *I shall be telling this with a sigh*
> *Somewhere ages and ages hence:*
> *Two roads diverged in a wood, and I—*
> *I took the one less travelled by,*
> *And that has made all the difference.*

When you maintain a balance in your thoughts, the difference would be of a positive context. You would be happy and at peace internally. There is one crucial thing about the balance. When you first discarded the training wheels, you would not have balanced your cycle immediately. You had to go through a process where you constantly experimented and made adjustments to find your grip.

You would have seen that cycling on an elevation is different from cycling on a flat road. There is no static position. You have to jostle for balance against counterbalancing and tipping yourself over constantly. It is a process needing constant re-evaluation.

Similarly, when you negotiate with the tensions in your life, you need to evaluate and re-evaluate your choices constantly.

With time you will realize that the path to greater satisfaction is not straightforward. You will have to weave in and out in response to different scenarios. If we were to revisit the example of career and family time, you might spend more time with your family on important dates like anniversaries and birthdays. Other weeks, you might spend more time working at the office. It is all about managing your growth.

Balance does not mean 50-50

There is also a misconception that balance means equal amounts of two things. That is not the case. It can mean doing only one thing but peppering it or having small doses of something else as well. It means that your life and actions are not unidimensional. Every once in a while, you will be expected to balance your behavior with diametrically opposite activities.

The Scottish novelist Robert Louis Stevenson once remarked, *"As if a man's soul were not too small, to begin with, they have dwarfed and narrowed theirs by a life of all work and no play; until here they are at forty, with a listless attention, a mind vacant of all material of amusement, and not one thought to rub against another, while they wait for the train."*

Stevenson said these words in 1877, a few decades after the Industrial Revolution. He talks of how a man living in the existence of his conventional occupation compromises on many other elements of his life. The world has changed since then, and as I remarked earlier, it has become even more complex and time-bound. The need for balance in this age could not be starker. However, there is no universal mix of activities that can be considered as the perfect balance. It is about finding the right mix for you. If we were to take the example of diets again, a balanced diet does not mean that you alternate every healthy meal with unhealthy food.

A balanced diet would probably feature one or two cheat meals in an entire week or fortnight's worth of meals—it is about finding the right mix. To extend the example further, the diet plan will also vary upon an individual's metabolism and Body Mass Index (BMI).

There can be no compromise regarding the law of the land; honesty—to yourself and the people around you, your character, and your conscience. There is no balance in these things. Here, there is no choice between right and wrong—there is only one right answer. And you had better be right for these dimensions all the time.

Through this book, I want to help you navigate through the contradictions in your life. Each of you is unique and comes with a different set of circumstances. I want to help you reflect and evaluate these tensions so that you can make the correct choice and attain the best balance.

I would also like to remind you that finding your balance is a process. It takes time and cannot be found in a moment. If I could extrapolate the cycling analogy further, here's an example of British cycling and Sir David Brailsford. David Brailsford became the head of British Cycling in 2002. At that juncture, Great Britain had only one gold medal in their 76 years of participation in the Olympics. Brailsford also later became the Performance Director of Team Sky, which later became a behemoth in the *Tour de France* under his stewardship.

However, it is his accomplishments with British cycling that saw him be knighted. After becoming the head of British cycling, Great Britain won two gold medals at the 2004 Athens Olympics. They also won seven out of the ten available gold medals in the 2008 Beijing Olympics. The same feat was repeated at home in the 2012 London Olympics. After he became the Performance Director at Team Sky in 2010, Brailsford once again showed his credentials.

Bradley Wiggins won the *Tour de France* within two years, becoming the first British cyclist to win the event. Team Sky bagged the trophy again in 2013, 2015, 2016, 2017 and 2018.

But what did he do? He prescribed to a theory of aggregation of marginal gains.

He focussed more on making the cyclist feel comfortable than on any innovation of technical components. All technical and equipment changes were driven by the need to make the cyclist comfortable. They experimented with ideas such as cycling outdoors with indoor clothing. They looked to standardize saddle heights. They even tested to see which pillows gave the competitors the best sleep and carried them to the events.

I want to extrapolate that idea and say that you just need to find the aggregation of reflection and balance. Finding your balance within these tensions will not be easy. However, I want you to feel comfortable when you challenge these tensions to find your way forward. You will see in one of the upcoming chapters the importance of optimism being discussed in detail. For now, remember that there will always be light at the end of the tunnel, and you must intend to walk towards it no matter how far away it may seem to be. This is the reason why I have written this book. I see people stumble in finding their balance. They look for immediate satisfaction, and some of them already have a considerable burden of regrets. They can constantly ask themselves if they have been fair in their dealings with others.

The world asks people to confront their pressures immediately. With this book, I hope to help you consider your pressures and contradictions. I want to help you live your life to its balanced potential.

So, before we proceed further, reflect on the life you have lived so far. Think of your greatest regrets and happiness. What were the dualities involved?

I'm sure you may have fantasized about the life you could have lived if you had opted for the other choice. Instead, what I want you to do is ask yourself how could you have navigated those two choices better? Could you have possibly found a middle ground?

Did spite inspire your decisions? Were your actions impulsive? Reflect on those choices and regrets. In this book, we shall explore the possible set of conflicts you are set to face in your professional and personal lives.

As you read through this book, I hope that you will find your balance and navigate all that life throws at you.

PART B
HARMONIZING THE
COUNTERFORCES

2
CONTRADICTIONS IN PROFESSIONAL LIFE

Our life is filled with contradictions and paradoxes. They require confrontation, and it is in this tension between two contrasting positions that we find success. When you learn to cycle, you learn to finely balance between the two forces that could see you fall on either side of the cycle.

Let us say you are at a new job and your boss welcomes you to the team. As you work for him/her, you realize that he/she is a generous boss. Soon you will find that your relationship has gone beyond the professional boundaries, and you have become friends. As time progresses, you see an opportunity to go to another company, but you may feel tied down by your relationship and loyalty to your boss.

If we were to take this example to the extreme, you see your boss commit a mistake. Will your loyalty and friendship hinder you from possibly confronting him/her about the issue?

These are just suppositions. However, you are bound by many such tensions. Oftentimes, you might let them fester as you may be apprehensive of confronting these tensions. If you wish to lead a better and balanced life, it is essential to identify where your tensions lie.

In this section, I have identified a set of tensions that apply to your professional life and another set that will apply to your personal life. There's also a set of tensions that could jointly affect your personal and professional life. The following tensions affect most of our professional careers. They are also a very challenging set of tensions that need deeper reflection to find your balance within them. They are:

1. Ambition to succeed vs. Being content
2. Being pushy vs. Being patient
3. Bursts of action vs. Downtime
4. Optimism vs. Readiness for the worst
5. Persistence vs. Knowing when to move on
6. Speaking vs. Listening
7. Individual credit vs. Team credit

Firstly, I will introduce each conflict using a scenario. I will then break it down to help you understand how these tensions may apply to you. At the end of every topic, I will list key summary points for review and reflection.

Take your time with each of these sections to see how they apply to your own life. You could then look to apply your learnings to address the tensions in your own respective lives. I also would like to stress that balance is never found in a static phase. There is no perfect equilibrium because the world around us is constantly moving. There is no balance in standing still. You need to keep swaying to move forward.

Some occasions will require you to lean towards one end, and there will be occasions when you must lean the other way. It is just like riding your bicycle. If you remain static, you will fall. But when you ride, there will be a constant but subtle movement to keep yourself upright and moving forward. Likewise, there is no perfect mid-point. You need to find what works for you and be dynamic to respond to any changes. We shall begin with the set of contradictions within your professional life. The first tension I would like to address is your desire to achieve more and consolidate your standing.

Ambition to succeed vs. Being content

Rahul always knew that he wanted to be wealthy. He was born into a middle-class family and went to a good school. Most of his classmates came from affluent families, and he saw them come in luxurious cars.

He also saw them owning some of the latest technological gadgets that his parents couldn't afford. He knew he wanted to be wealthy and worked hard for it. He ensured that he got good grades and got into a top engineering school.

During his engineering course, he started preparing for a management entrance exam. He aspired to get into one of the top management schools in the country, and he did. He also got an opportunity to work abroad, and he took it.

In the first five years, Rahul amassed a lot of wealth due to the time he put into his work and his thrifty nature. He was working close to 18 hours a day.

Rahul then got an opportunity to look for fresh career prospects. He had two offers. One gave him a significant pay rise, but the work hours were equally brutal with a lot more responsibilities. The other offer came with more flexible work hours, but the salary was lower than his current salary.

What: Rahul finds himself at a crossroads. One: Increase his wealth but with a lot more stress. Two: Take up a less demanding job but with a lower pay packet. Rahul knows that the first option will give him a fatter bank balance, while the second option will allow him to relax and catch up on the various life moments he has missed out on over the years.

Who: It is clear that Rahul has been motivated by the perceived lack of resources due to his background. He has single-mindedly chosen the path where he could make the most money. He opted for courses and jobs that would pay him the most. He didn't relax and worked hard to earn the big bucks.

Where and When: It is up to Rahul to make a choice. Can he keep up the grueling work schedule? His thrifty nature means that he has saved up a lot of money. When will he seek to enjoy the fruits of his labor? These are the decisions that Rahul has to make.

How: Rahul chose this life influenced by the material possessions of his peers during his school days. It is an innate hunger that is driving his actions to accumulate as much money as he can. Such hunger will never die; it leaves an individual wanting more no matter how wealthy he already is. Understand this. There is no point in accumulating wealth if a person does not enjoy it in the later years of his life. His life will turn out to be a perfect summation of the poem *Leisure* by William Henry Davies:

> "...*A poor life this if, full of care,*
> *We have no time to stand and stare.*"

Why: It is inevitable that you want to succeed at your workplace. Companies may evaluate you based on the deals you secure for them. Your accomplishments in the professional sphere define your success. You know that the world is generally result-oriented, and every one of us has a desire to succeed. It could be motivated by different factors.

Chiefly, we all want to find ourselves at a better place than where we find ourselves today. We should constantly strive to improve. We must have that gumption to succeed. It is critical. However, temper that fire with the knowledge that there are unfortunate people in this world who don't even possess a fraction of your belongings.

I am not reminding you of this fact to show you any difference between you and the underprivileged. I want you to recognize your fortune and luck. You need to take time to thank God for all the good things and blessings that He has bestowed upon you. You were lucky to be born in a family that could afford your education. It is providence that you were born into the right family as the family's status determines the future life of an infant.

If you were born to a family where you couldn't afford to go to school, would you have found yourself in the same position as you are now, even if you put the same effort or more?

So, you may ask, how do I proceed here? You have two options. In the first option, you could opt to make extra money and accumulate the stress that comes with the job. The other option would be to make enough money. It may not let you lead an opulent and decadent lifestyle. But you will surely live a good life. I am not recommending that you curb your ambitions. I'm just asking you to be grateful that you have the chance to dream and then nurture it.

Ambition to succeed
- Easy to get sidetracked by societal standards of "success".
- Measuring one's worth in terms of money.

Being content
- Focused on improvement of oneself rather than competing with others.
- Weighing your achievements in terms of hard-work and effort rather than materialistic ideals.

Why is it important that we be grateful for our opportunities? The first thing we need to understand is our current world. It is a highly materialistic world, and we measure success in economic terms.

Right from your childhood, you would have found yourself being compared to students who score higher grades. If you were to enter a college, you would find that your efforts will be concentrated more on grades. Your grades will help determine the interest of the few top companies that can give you handsome pay packets.

If you were to notice, even when you find a job via college placements, the perception of the best job is generally determined by the size of the pay packet rather than the circumstances of the job.

People rarely stop to examine the growth potential and other related circumstances with the job. This is the reason why many people find themselves dissatisfied with their jobs. There used to be a time when being a well-paid doctor or engineer was considered a success. Then came the IT boom. Now there is the occupation of big data analysts. You may adopt any path to success, but ensure that it is an honest one. Be aggressive in your pursuit of excellence but never compromise on your honesty and integrity.

One way to find the balance between ambition and contentment would be to look via the prism of your age. When you are younger, you have more energy and fire. You will have the time to commit to longer hours as you are not yet entrusted with familial responsibilities. However, with age, you will be expected to shoulder a lot more. You may be married and with children. This would mean that you have shared responsibility for your immediate family.

You may also be worried about your bills or the mortgage payment due along with these other responsibilities. You need to understand that ambition to succeed is mostly driven by material goals. This pursuit can be endless. You could scale a peak only to see a taller one looking down on you. You will find that this would be an endless pursuit. Additionally, you could also be burdened by unnecessary competition. The size of your wallet would decide your worth. This could lead to a lot of uncomfortable situations like jealousy.

To counter this endless loop, you need to learn to be content. I agree that it is easier said than done, especially when you are younger. The maturity to determine what is enough will only come with age. When you grow older, you will be conscious of the futility of the chase while recognizing that you still have to play the game. Contentment does not mean lethargy. However, it is a feeling that comes from within you.

You can only attain such a state when you are truly at peace with yourself. When you reach such a level of comfort, you will find that you will no longer be motivated by jealousy. I want to caution once more that you cannot claim to be content when you are lazy.

I'm reminded of another Swami Vivekananda quote, which goes: *"You can forgive only when you are in a position of being able to forgive. Otherwise, it is cowardice."* You can only claim to be content when you earn it with your dedication and commitment to work. One way to strike a balance between the two is to compete with yourself and not with somebody else.

Suppose most of your actions are to improve yourself (your habits, discipline, intellect, expertise in an area, attitude…), rather than to impress others, you will be fine in terms of balancing the two aforementioned forces. You will value the improvements you have made in your life, as you know fully well how difficult they have been to accomplish; there is automatic contentment that comes in. So, you need to constantly motivate yourself, have the drive and ambition, bring in a degree of being content and then be ambitious again.

Points to ponder and reflect upon

- Try to achieve a lot more when you are younger; try to achieve things before assuming broader familial responsibilities.
- As you age, you will realize that a certain amount of money is enough to live a comfortable lifestyle. Always look at the people who aren't as privileged as you and thank your stars for the life you're living.
- Compete with yourself. Do not compare your situation with that of others.
- Be courageous. You should be able to kickstart your life even if you lose everything and must gain everything from scratch. Having this mindset will also keep your ego in check!

One of the key factors when you join a company is your ambition. Companies naturally treasure go-getters. So, it is understandable when you would like to be more ambitious. Find your balance by considering the points just discussed.

However, if you were to speak about ambition, there needs to be a conversation about two particular attitudes at work. You could either be a gregarious and impatient one or a reticent one. Each attitude has its pros and cons. So, when you are chasing your ambition, you could be persistent. Some may even refer to it as 'being pushy.' You could also be very self-confident about your skillset and prefer to be patient.

Being pushy vs. Being patient

Mark and George are two mid-level management employees at a company. Their boss will be retiring at the end of the year. The gossip is that the company will be looking to promote from within rather than headhunt an executive from another company. Mark and George know that they need to step up their work to be noticed. They are also trying to sign a partnership deal with two key potential businesses. They know that inking their respective deals would go a long way in their promotion prospects.

Mark picks up the more ambitious deal. He brings his team together and asks them to be prepared for overtime in the coming days. He toils along with his team and prepares what they consider to be a sure-fire deal-winning presentation. Mark then meets up with the decision-makers of the potential client. He presents with gusto and charm.

He reinforces the key points, and he can see that the people seem visibly impressed. He then takes them out to a 5-star hotel and treats them to wine and dinner. They have a wonderful interaction. They part with Mark telling him that they would be in touch. He gets a few informal messages thanking him for that evening. Mark is sure that he has got this in the bag.

But there is radio silence for the next two days. Mark gets so antsy that he wants to bombard his contact with e-mails and calls. Unable to resist, he makes one phone call. It goes unanswered.

He then calls the office number, gets the secretary, and leaves a message asking for an update.

What: It is clear that Mark wants the promotion. There are two obvious paths here:

- **Option 1:** Mark could bombard the contact with follow-up messages. Every unanswered response could drive him to push the ante further. He could keep up this relentlessness until he gets his desired result.

- **Option 2:** He could patiently wait for a response. He could trust that his presentation and the brand capital of his organization would be enough to persuade his potential client.

Both seem viable methods, and he could land the client. However, there could be some unintended consequences. If he chose the first option, he could have come across as 'pushy,' which could annoy his contact and thus the client. If he chose the second option, he could also lose the client if he has competition. Somebody else could have a better pitch in terms of cost or Return on Investment (ROI) and could have been more persistent in their efforts to convince the client.

Who: Mark's actions are going to be driven by his desire to get the promotion. If he chose the first option, he could be driven by a desperation to land the client. He could be like a horse with a bit between its teeth. He would want regular updates and follow-ups. When his desperation drives his actions, he will not be able to examine them in a rational light. If he chooses the second option, he might do so to portray a position of calmness and strength. He would want the client desperately, but he doesn't want to show his cards.

Where and When: Both these options are two extremes. The best way to approach this scenario is to adopt a mixture of pushiness and patience. Mark will have to tailor his approach based on the depth of his relationship with his contact. If they are close, he will be able to push more. If they aren't, he will have to start by being patient and then slowly get pushy.

How: The first step would be to build and establish one's credibility. Mark should use the presentation to showcase his credibility. He should be indirectly pushy by reminding his clients of his past successes and the company's many merits. His communication should feature a lot of soft signals reinforcing these credentials.

The next step would be to be patient. When you wait for an update, it also builds up respect for your position. When there is no response, and you feel that you have been patient for a good amount of time, you can start being pushy—this time, you need not resort to indirect signals and be persistent in chasing your lead.

Patience is a virtue prescribed by many. However, business is about time. You need to find the right balance for yourself. Some opportunities can't be missed, and you need to pursue them diligently. However, this does not discount the importance of patience.

In this day and age, it is easy to get distracted and chase the next big thing. You need the patience to stick to one lane for a period of time. Patience is necessary to focus. My first job was at OPNET in Washington DC. I loved the company and the work that I did. My colleagues were warm and generous. On all counts, it was a dream job. I took the first project to establish myself in the company. It was a great project, and I used it to plant my roots firmly within the company in the first couple of years.

Once I felt that I had built a stable foundation, I looked to push outwards into broader consulting work areas with clients I was interested in. If I were to look at my career, I have chosen a mix of being patient and persistent. However, the events that made all the difference were borne out of slam-dunking the opportunities I had created by my persistence.

Why: It is necessary to keep moving out of these phases. You can't be spending too much time in any of these extremes. If you do, you will be either considered to be pushy or laidback. A mixture of both will be a better reflection of your personality to the people around you.

If you ever find yourself confused between the two choices, it is better to err on the side of being patient. Let us consider some of the cases where you will find yourself in this conundrum. You could have just joined a new workplace or academic institution. Or you might be feeling stuck at your current job, and you don't feel happy about how things have been unfolding. You will find yourself with the choice to either stick or make a change. I would recommend you to be patient as time will allow things to sort themselves out. I understand that this is easier said than done. Whenever I opted to be patient, I've repeated the maxim, "*whatever happens, happens for the best!*" to myself whenever I doubted my choice.

Patience is essential as people can be easily swayed by their immediate mood. They are liable to have a knee-jerk reaction. What you need is the distance to look at the broader picture than your immediate feelings. Evaluate your position rationally. When you contemplate your circumstances calmly, you will find the answer for yourself. "*Life is not a sprint; it is a marathon. So be conservative till you are well past the mid-way stage.*" As I said earlier, by being patient, you are trying to cool the heat of the situation. However, to be patient, you need confidence, and you need to avoid the feelings of loss and the fears of missing out on opportunities. When you opt to be patient, you know that this is the best-case scenario. You will find your balance in that acceptance. You should be patient with the understanding that you are ready to push forward and claim your space once the situation changes in your favor.

You must have the foundations to be patient. You need to be ready to push when the situation demands. The best way to lay that foundation lies in your ability to achieve small wins and make progress.

This progress is about establishing yourself so that you have the credibility to push later on. Do not confuse patience with laziness. Patience does not mean that you can sit back and relax. You still need to pay attention to your surroundings. There are many learning opportunities around you. I cannot stress this enough – take those opportunities.

So, when you are given a pitch, get your head around it. Examine them thoroughly and analyze every detail. You can only do so when you take your time to understand the nitty-gritty details.

Being pushy
- Belief that if you do not ask/insist, you might not get it.
- May overwhelm someone to prove your credibility.

Being patient
- Believing in your work and waiting for the right time to voice what you want.
- Achieving small wins and being consistent with your work.

Patience could also mean that you wait for the other person to tire out or the system to fix itself. Everything is a system of sorts; people, processes, emotions, data, and divergent goals all come together to make the machine work. For example, your role in the workplace is subject to all of these forces, from yourself to the industry you are in, to your manager, and your peers. For things to fall into place, especially after putting in your effort, you need to wait it out. When you opt to be patient, you learn that the system responds favorably to you. You might also find a comfortable level and position which is apt for you.

One of the best examples of this strategy comes from sport. Steven Bradbury, an Australian ice speed skater, won the 2002 Winter Olympics Gold medal based on the strategy of patience. He expected and hoped that the front runners would crumble.

He held back and didn't put himself into the leading pack. He hung around the back, and just before the finish line, one of the leaders slipped, causing a chain reaction. His fall would lead to all of the front runners crashing on the home stretch. This crash would open up a free lane for Bradbury to skate into first place after avoiding the earlier fracas.

However, when you push, you mustn't project an image of impatience. There is a difference between persistence and impatience. Pushy is also good because if you don't ask, you don't get it. However, you need to know when to ask and how to ask. By this nature, you need to develop a certain degree of comfort in the system before you decide on being pushy. Because, with familiarity comes the sense of knowing when and how to make that push. Also, you will know the norms of what is acceptable and what is not in the environment before being pushy.

That familiarity comes with patience. Hence, it is important to be patient first. The next time you find it difficult to be patient, look at any of Rahul Dravid's test innings. There is a reason they call him 'The Wall.' Learn the virtue of being patient with the system and your opposition. Sometimes just standing your ground is also a sign of being pushy. You do not need to create a ruckus to get the attention.

Points to ponder and reflect upon

- Generally, it is better to err on the side of patience.
- Patience does not equate to laziness; you have to be constantly alert to move when you find yourself in favorable circumstances. *"Luck is what happens when preparation meets opportunity."* – Seneca.
- However, you can only afford to be patient when you have the credibility to do so (hence, small wins help).
- Sometimes, you have to push for what you want for if you don't fight for it, chances are no one else will.

When you find yourself in a hyper-competitive world that values accomplishments, you will find yourself in a race against time. There are many tasks to do and not enough time. One of the more prevalent terms used in corporate circles is 'burnout.' One of the drawbacks of being in a persistence-based strategy is the requirement of inexhaustible stamina. However, we as human beings, are not machines with such a trait.

The constant stress to be ahead can be quite telling on the human psyche. Burnout is a state where one is emotionally, mentally, and physically exhausted. This state is caused due to prolonged stress and the failure to manage it. This leads to the question of how do you manage such stress? One prescribed method is the balancing of work time and personal time. In countries like Germany, there are schemes in place to get a week off at saunas for people to focus on themselves. However, these are not available universally. But as the term burnout gained significance, another term too grew in stature: 'downtime.' But how important is downtime, and how much downtime can you afford?

Bursts of action vs. Downtime

Neha was headhunted by a company to head the Planning and Strategy department. The previous head was retiring by the end of the week. He had invited Neha to give her a background of the job and the team. As they sat discussing the work, Neha was told to take care of another relatively new hire, Ramesh. He was a go-getter and the best person on the team. However, Neha was warned that he seemed to have boundless energy for work. Neha later checked the files and reports of her potential team. It was clear that Ramesh was among the fastest to complete his goals and move on to the next project. She also saw from the time logs that he was usually the first to enter the office and the last to leave. He also worked during some holidays. On her first day, Neha called Ramesh into her office. He gave a progress report and said that he was going to embark on a new project. Neha told him to leave that to another team member and to take a week's paid leave. She wanted him to relax and then come back. Ramesh was distraught and tried to say that he didn't need a break and could still work effectively.

What: Ramesh has been working indefatigably to achieve his goals. Neha can see that he has spared no efforts to remain at the front of his projects.

However, she has also noticed that he works longer than others to remain effective. While his speed is among the best, his hours are also longer than his teammates per project.

Who: Ramesh feels that his hard work has been punished. He has lost a project that he had already worked on and planned. He feels like his leave will affect his work. However, Neha can see that his efficiency has gone down. His longer hours have masked the problems with his work. She does identify him as a good professional. But she wants him with a cooler head to avoid any potential burnout.

Where and When: Neha wants him to take breaks as she wants him to reflect on his work. His boundless energy has meant that he has not taken the time to investigate the reasons for his long hours. He could be making mistakes or not planning for any potential pitfalls before he proceeded to complete his project.

How: Ramesh needs to take breaks and reflect. He should look to recharge by doing things that he may love. He must take a break. He could just relax by taking the time to do things that he didn't have the time to do earlier. During the last couple of days, he could think of what he needs to do when he returns to work. He could calmly think about it without the pressures of deadlines.

Why: Let us first explore why downtime is important. I'm sure you have heard of the phrase, 'engine overheating.' Even machines need to cool down in order to work efficiently. When they are stretched beyond their limits, they can snap and malfunction. Similarly, in a human context, I believe that that excellence comes from a calm mind. Your brain needs to be calm and rational to make the best decisions. So, you must create opportunities for the mind to rest. I know it can be quite addictive to knock off your goals as quickly as possible. However, there is something deceptive about speed. It can narrow your vision and make you ignore everything else.

The addictive rush of completing your goals will also be subject to the law of diminishing returns. Every successful feat will feel less special, and you will start to grow cynical. This cynicism will only lead to burnout. Hence, you must create situations for the mind to relax. Some examples could be regular exercises, early morning walks, calm and long drives without the hassle of traffic, open conversations with family, a quiet time for reflection and recuperation. Downtime does not mean only vacations. It is the periods of 'lull' that you can create for yourself during your work weeks and days.

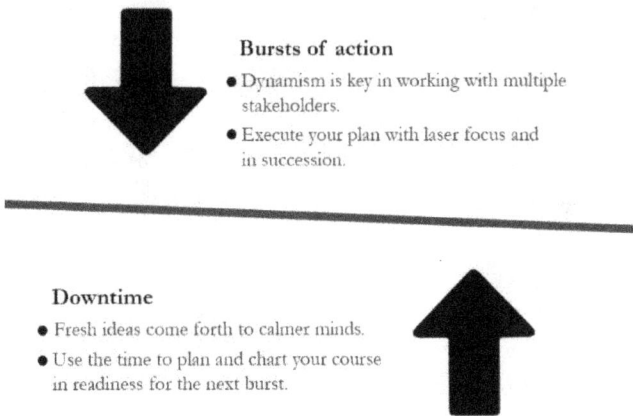

Bursts of action

- Dynamism is key in working with multiple stakeholders.
- Execute your plan with laser focus and in succession.

Downtime

- Fresh ideas come forth to calmer minds.
- Use the time to plan and chart your course in readiness for the next burst.

When you give yourself this break, you allow fresh ideas to flood your mind. You can then explore these ideas, expand them, and optimize them. When you are calmer, your vision will expand to take in the surroundings. When your vision isn't hyper-narrow on the goal, you could see the potential snags that could affect it. You could then plan for these snags and possible consequences.

You will have a Plan B or even a Plan C to counter any of these potential pitfalls. When you are calmer, you will recognize the multiple stakeholders involved in the plan. So, when you plan, you will realize that there is a fine art in keeping the multiple stakeholders happy. You will only recognize these elements when you are rational and methodical in your planning. Once you have drawn up a careful plan, then execute it with full steam!

Set up milestones and deadlines to achieve them. You can then go on a burst of action and accomplish your goals. Your burst of action is best done when you have planned, and you know exactly what needs to get done. Thus, do not plan in haste. It is antithetical to the very meaning of the word 'plan.'

You need to create the time for downtime. You need the time to recharge your batteries. The opportunity to relax does not just fall into your lap. I'm sure you have seen people plan it out in their planners. They will have days allotted to take a break, like a bike trip to a hill station or a holiday with family. When you take these opportunities to relax, you can start charting the path for the next set of objectives. You have to cycle between the two. If you only opt for downtime, you will become lethargic and not achieve anything.

Points to ponder and reflect upon

- You need a period of rest to recharge your mind and reflect.
- Plan when you are calm as only then can you see the broader picture.
- You need to shift between phases where you burst into action and phases where you take the downtime; you will burn out if you are constantly working. And if you only opt for downtime, you will become lethargic.
- When you are calm, both physically and mentally, your mind is getting the time to think. And when you think, you lay out your plan and execute the task with double speed!

As I mentioned earlier, when you plan with a rational mind, you will see the potential pitfalls. This broad overview is essential for success. However, such carefulness can overreach into negativity and pessimism. People are capable of so much more than what cold, emotionless logic can dictate. Human ingenuity and spirit are intangibles for which you cannot account when you draw up a plan. But how much can you rely on such intangible qualities, and how careful can you be to the limit where you come across as pessimistic?

Optimism vs. Readiness for the worst

John is the CEO of a start-up. He has opened an online store for delivering organic produce in a metropolitan city. He sources his produce from the local farmers around the city and delivers the ordered goods within a day. He started his company with two of his friends. They planned to become successful in their launch city and then expand to other urban areas. In the first year, they made a tidy profit. The two friends also expanded to non-meat alternatives, packed foods and more. These items were a success as well. The two friends then talked with John regarding their expansion plans.

There was already a sizeable social media presence for the business. Many people from neighboring cities had asked them to expand into their areas as well. The two friends wanted to expand immediately. John, however, was circumspect about their prospects. He wanted to consolidate their position first. He also argued that social media likes didn't translate into actual orders.

What: John finds himself in a progressive company. While it is profitable, he wants the company to establish itself in its launch city firmly. He does not see it as the ripe time for expansion.

Who: There are two clear positions. John is cautious and does not believe that social media engagements are a true barometer to test the market demand.

He feels that the company still needs to find its footing firmly. His two friends, meanwhile, want to expand. They have also been bolstered by the success of alternative products they helped launch in the original city. They have also found encouragement in social media engagements.

Where and When: John will have to either convince his friends that their position is not yet firm in their launch city or look at the demand in the neighboring city. He will have to draw up a timeline with specific goals which need to be met before expansion.

How: If John draws up a timeline, he will need specific goals. What is this firm position that he considers will be stable enough for expansion?

What are the challenges and possible pitfalls he foresees? He needs to strategize for these challenges. If he plans to expand immediately, how will he conduct his market research? Who will be his suppliers, and how will he address logistical issues? Essentially, he needs a plan.

Why: Whenever you look to achieve a goal, you need a plan and have a timeline. The timeline is ideally a long-term one as it gives you the time to accomplish your goals. As mentioned earlier, your progress can be affected by dynamic changes. When you plan, you need to account for all these types of changes.

Ideally, when you plan according to a timeline, it is vital that you set short and medium-term goals. These milestones will be your guiding markers for the plan. So, you would be planning on how to knock these goals and have accomplished your objectives at the end of the projected timeline.

Within those plans, you should have a set of backup plans ready for specific parts where you feel the original plan could break down. When you arrange for these backup plans, you are keeping yourself 'plan-proofed.' So, how would one know which parts of the plan need backup? One must assume that something will go wrong in any or all parts of the plan and that backup plans are needed around those pitfalls.

Before we proceed, let us first define a short-term plan and a medium-term plan. Your short-term plans are for one to three months, and the medium-term plans are for a year. However, as I mentioned earlier, you need time to relax and also do other activities. These goals should not take up all your time.

You will have to budget for your regular activities. You need to find the schedule to include these activities along with your short-term and medium-term goals. We shall explore the idea of planning your schedule in a later chapter.

"There are really two kinds of optimism. There's the complacent, Pollyanna optimism that says, 'Don't worry - everything will be just fine,' and that allows one to just lay back and do nothing about the problems around you. Then there's what we call dynamic optimism. That's an optimism based on action."
— *Ramez Naam.*

The assumption that anything can go wrong does not mean that one cannot afford to be optimistic. It is vital as you need a positive mindset to progress positively. You need that mindset to face the challenges that will be thrown at you. When you set your short and medium-term goals, as an optimist, you will see good things unfold. Your optimism must be infused in the tasks you do to accomplish your short and medium-term goals. Ensure that you have certain goals that you actually want to accomplish. They should be goals that you look forward to completing. The personal satisfaction you experience when you achieve those goals will keep you going in the long term. They will motivate you to stay on the path.

Even when things go wrong, if you have planned for it, you will see that no form of negativity will pollute your mind and actions. Thus, it is essential to temper optimism with paranoia. Always expect the worst so that you can prepare for it. It would be best to follow the example of Benjamin Disraeli, who said, *"I am prepared for the worst, but hope for the best."* When you prepare for the worst, you will know that you are covered for any eventuality.

When you believe that you are indeed covered for any eventuality, it will boost your confidence to greater heights. Let us say, for example, you bought a house, and you needed to take a mortgage to buy it. The optimistic view would be that you would be able to meet your monthly mortgage payments and that with your current job prospects and potential salary raises, you would be able to close the loan early. That viewpoint is optimistic. If you temper it with cautiousness, you will realize that you need to have a buffer in case of any emergency. What if you lose your job? What if any immediate family member has a medical emergency requiring heavy expenditure?

What if you default on the loan – what are your options? What will be the backup plans for these circumstances? If you plan for these backups, what are the current risks and costs involved? These are the things you need to plan for. So, while you must stretch and buy that house (ambition and optimism), do not lose sight of the worst-case scenarios so that you can cover for it.

Optimism
- Positive reinforcement drives people to do better.
- Optimism is contagious; people around will reflect it back.
- When you believe positively about something, it will motivate you to achieve it.

Readiness for the worst
- Being optimistic without giving it enough effort will most likely result in failure.
- When one has prepared for every situation, the rate of success will be higher.

When you are in a leadership position, you need to reflect boundless optimism. Your team members will turn to you for cues in case of setbacks. Thus, when you plan for worst-case scenarios, you need not share them with the people around you—prepare for the worst in your mind. But, share the optimistic spirit with the people around you.

Positive reinforcement is what drives people to strive and do better. So, share the positive thoughts with your staff and be private about your backup plans. What is the difference between ambition and optimism? Optimists in situations will see and look at the positive side. They will expect the good playing out.

Ambitious people are people who are striving to stretch themselves and achieve more. They are the ones who are ready to push through no matter what the battle might reveal. Failure is not a dead-end, instead a place to pause and re-strategize and move forward with grace. They set bold, audacious goals and achieve them.

So, if you find yourself struggling for optimism, don't be worried.

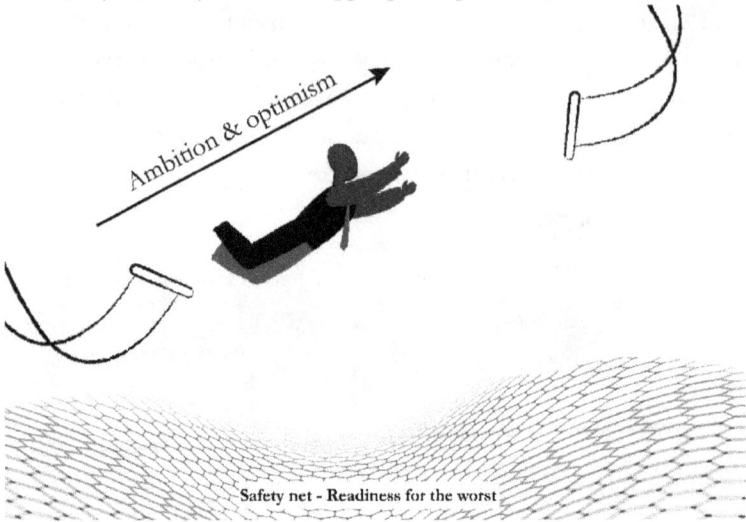

It is not a switch that you can turn on and off as per your will. If you find yourself cautious more often, take heart in the fact that you are covered for most eventualities and consequences.

Points to ponder and reflect upon

- Optimism is a must to keep you on the road; it drives you forward.
- Cautiousness is equally important so that you can respond effectively to the challenges thrown at you.
- Plan for the long-term goal with a set of short-term and medium-term objectives. Draw up your game plans to knock these objectives and have a set of backup game plans for any potential pitfalls.

As you plan forward, you will realize with time that your environment is dynamic and can change at the drop of a hat. On occasions like this, you will come across certain forks on the road. You cannot ideally plan for such conundrums as each situation needs to be judged on its own merit.

One such issue could be whether to stick or switch. There will be certain occasions when the grass seems greener on the other side. Should you jump or should you stay?

Persistence vs. Knowing when to move on

Nitin has been trying to land an account which he believes will net his company a huge profit. However, he has competition from other companies to land the account.

Nitin has spent many hours familiarizing himself with the potential client. He also believes that his presentation has been the best. However, he hasn't gotten a firm answer from the client. He feels that they are playing all sides of the game and are trying to garner the most benefits.

It is at this juncture that he becomes aware of another possible client. He knows that many people, including those at his company and his competition, are currently unaware of this opportunity.

What: Nitin can see that he has two options here. He can stick to his current project and ensure that his hard work comes to fruition. He can only do so if he gives up on the new opportunity or lets someone else handle it. He can't make a firm decision as he is unsure about either of them.

Who: It is clear that Nitin doesn't want to lose the opportunity to distinguish himself. Landing either client can be a feather in his cap. However, he has spent a lot of time on the first potential client. In the case of the second potential client, he will have to do everything from scratch.

Where and When: Nitin can grab the new opportunity if he wants. He may also have to face competition when people realize that he has moved to a new client. This could affect his relationship with the first potential client. However, he also feels that his current discussions with the latter have not been progressing well.

10

How: Nitin must weigh both the options. He has to investigate if the second potential client can net him the same gains or better the existing ones. How sure is he that he can land the first account? Has he given enough time for the first project? Is his desire to move on motivated by his frustration with the first potential client for their delayed response? If it is driven by frustration, it could just be a case of "grass is greener on the other side." He may face the same problems with the second project as well.

Why: It is important to know when you should move on and when you should keep persisting. This does not mean that you should move on whenever you hit a wall. Careers are short, and opportunities are fleeting. When you find yourself stuck, you need to work on it and not jump at the first available opportunity.

When you give up too easily, you will be left with many 'what-ifs' at the end of your career. It would be best to remember the effort and time you put in to build a solid foundation. Capitalize on it. More often than not, your desire to move on or persist may sometimes be driven by your own ego.

You may feel slighted when someone doesn't respond to your overtures and efforts. On the other hand, you may feel that by persisting, you are being firm in your beliefs and standing up for them. There is no easy answer to finding the sweet spot within this tension. You should have no illusions that this type of scenario will be a one-off. You will be subjected to this tension throughout your career.

If you are looking to negotiating this tension within the context of your entire career, you will need to first break it down into few stages. I'm sure you have heard of the phrase "thinking from the mind" and "thinking from the heart." This phrase can be translated to working from the heart and working from the mind in a professional sphere.

So, in the earliest phase of your career, work from your heart. Let your passion and energy be seen. As you progress, pick up the skills you need to develop further.

Learn them from observation and insights you get from your peers. Once you pick up the skills, you can balance the working from your mind or heart based on the circumstances. I need to stress that you should avoid knee-jerk reactions. Knee jerk reactions are the reactions you commit without (extensive) thinking. A decision made without much consideration or by impulse might lead to regrets, and there might not be any way to undo it. They are especially important if your ego feels hurt whenever you are ignored.

Persistence
- You have to capitalize on the foundations built.
- Time can be a great healer.
- Knee-jerk reactions = Regrets.

Knowing when to move on
- Is my time being invested well?
- Is there a better opportunity?

If you ever need to get inspiration, I'll ask you to turn once again to cricket. Watch how Rahul Dravid constructed his innings. There is even a *YouTube* clip[3] showing him unruffled when he goes scoreless for 40 balls. He remains solid in his defense and plays every ball on its merit. He looks to tire the opposition bowler out and then capitalizes on it for scoring opportunities.

When you are in for the long innings, get settled in well. There will be occasions where you will be frustrated and annoyed; you cannot avoid this. The key is not to let them affect your work. Remember to give it enough thought; sleep on it before you feel like you're ready to deal with it. Many times, it is just about waiting it out. "Time is a great healer." Occasionally, misunderstandings are at the root of the issue. If you feel that is the case, seek clarification.

---

[3] https://www.youtube.com/watch?v=EIsc_8mxnkc

You may need to give time for the issue to settle. You have to believe that in time the real intentions and meanings will reveal themselves. I think most times, we tend to overestimate the severity of the situation and overreact correspondingly. Of course, it is not easy to pick this mentality immediately. You will need at least a couple of long projects to understand the finer details. Work from your heart on these projects. As you work, look for opportunities to pick the brains of your superiors at work. Understand how to identify the project's scope, contours, and gamut and your role within it. This will help you mature both functionally and as a leader.

The common-sense approach is to move only when you find a better opportunity than the current one. The thumb rule to follow when you consider moving on is to see if the new opportunity checks more boxes for you than your current one. However, you should only consider moving on if you have given more than enough time for the current project. If you feel that you have given more than enough time, ask yourself: Is my time being invested well? Is there something better I can do with my time? When you ponder upon these questions, you will find your answer if you work in a highly argumentative environment.

Do you find yourself being absent mentally even when you are physically present at your workplace? Do you enjoy your job? If you are saying 'yes' to these questions, then ask yourself if it is a phase. You could look to balance it with activities like exercise, doing good deeds, or spending time with your family. However, as I mentioned earlier, even though your answer might be a 'yes', if you have given enough time to it, then move on. Do not move on just because you are frustrated with the current project.

Points to ponder and reflect upon

- Don't jump at the first opportunity just because you find yourself at an impasse.
- In the early stages of your career, let your energy and enthusiasm shine through; look for opportunities to learn and develop.

- If you feel stuck and are sure that you have given enough time to untangle the issues, always ask yourself two questions before you consider moving on: Is my time being invested well? Can I do something better with my time?

This brings us to one of the most important elements within the professional sphere, human interaction. Human beings are social creatures, and we crave support, understanding, well-being, and entertainment with our contact with each other. With the advent of the digital age, the skill of communication has become radically important. Communication in the professional sphere is vital to avoid any snags or misunderstandings. There are many courses on business communication and how to communicate effectively. I would like to address one fundamental tension with the basic elements of communication: Speaking and listening.

Speaking vs. Listening

Allan and Brian have been invited to a strategy meeting. Their company is planning to expand into a new market with a new product. Their company has been producing goods for skin care and hair care for women. They want to expand into men's skincare and hair care. Allan and Brian have been brought into the room as they have been the leading salespeople since the previous year. They have the largest base of contacts in the market. They are also fundamentally different. Allan is more reticent but closes most sales. He has a base of contacts who regularly buy only from him. Brian is more exuberant and has the second-most sales. Brian, however, has a more varied base of contacts.

As the meeting starts, they are asked about the viability of expanding into men's skincare and hair care. Brian is quick to reply and talks of how men already use the current products and how any expansion will only be beneficial. He relates to the conversations he has had with shopkeepers and customers. Once Brian's lengthy exposition is over, Allan is asked for his opinion.

He, however, asks for more details on the potential product. When provided with more information, Allan asks for more time to consult with his contacts to answer more accurately.

What: A company is looking to expand and has asked its two leading salespeople for initial impressions on the viability of such an expansion. One of them is effusive in its prospects, and the other is cautious. The former also elaborates by talking up prospects from his many conversations, while the latter is generally silent, preferring to talk only when prodded.

Who: Brian is talkative. He makes references to his client conversations and explains them in detail. He is clearly bullish in his opinion and makes it clear. Allan's words carry a lot of weight. He clearly listens and wants to know what type of products will be part of the expansion and wants to look at the situation specifically rather than just a general overview.

Where and When: These are two contrasting approaches. Brian lets people know where he stands and is the first one to reply; he can keep the conversation going. He talks and brings up the many discussions he has held with clients to support his stand. Allan is not as talkative and only provides his answers when prodded. He prefers to listen and then offer his opinion to a specific question.

How: Both approaches have their benefits and drawbacks. Brian's enthusiasm can be key in selling the new products to potential new customers. His presentation is direct. While his speech may be long, he never deviates from the soul of the subject.

However, this enthusiasm can also be driven by a lack of actual ground reportage. He may not be listening closely and only heard what he wanted to hear.

Allan, on the other hand, is more measured. He needs his time to get his head around the question. However, his lack of enthusiasm may also send the wrong signals.

Why: Listening is always an underrated and undervalued skill. Always balance your speaking with abundant doses of listening. However, you should be listening in the active form. As Stephen R Covey said, *"Most people do not listen with the intent to understand; they listen with the intent to reply."*

Listen to understand and comprehend, not to respond. When you actually listen, you are opening up your mind to various perspectives. When you listen, you not only display an open mind but also reflect empathy and compassion. When you listen actively, you also reduce the chances of any miscommunications or misunderstandings. However, this is not to say that speaking up for yourself and your beliefs is not correct. When you speak, you will be able to establish your position. The best way to do so would be to speak in the first couple of minutes in a meeting to establish your position. This will put your perspective in focus, and then you can listen to others respond to it. I'm only warning against the possibility of such a habit clouding your rational mind.

So, when you establish your position, look to how others respond. Their responses could open up a fresh perspective that you might not have considered earlier. Your speaking and presentation style will matter when you are at the beginning of your career or education. How effective are you in your communication? To be effective, you should know how to be concise and keep your points crisp and clear. Your communication needs to be direct and without any scope for misinterpretation. It should be simple for the listener to tune into the wavelength of the idea you wish to convey. Do not unnecessarily use jargon to show off your expansive vocabulary. Imagine if you found yourself in a highly esoteric conversation. It will be tricky to contribute to that conversation.

Hence, keep your speech simple and clear. The only way you can ensure this is by understanding what you are trying to convey. If you are unclear about the message, your communication will also be equally vague. So, first, try and understand what you wish to convey. Have a firm grip on the subject. When you do so, you will be able to resonate with your listener.

Speaking
- Establishes your position.
- Your intentions and directions are clear to the team.

Listening
- Bring other perspectives into a discussion.
- Sign of empathy and compassion.
- Team player.

As you mature in your career, look to hone and develop your listening skills. Try and understand the other perspectives in play. Digest what others have to say. Such feedback will help in boosting team camaraderie and spirit. From my personal experience, I have found that speaking is very tiring! When you get comfortable with silence, it will help you gain inner peace. Silence affords you the chance to reflect and think deeply about the situation. I mentioned listening actively earlier. Do you know what active listening entails?

It is not just about keeping your ears open and listening to what someone says. It is about comprehending their speech. How do you do that? Keep your eyes and mind open and observe for non-verbal clues like body language and the tone of speech. Another positive consequence of active listening is that your memory works better. When you listen actively, your brain gets a head start – you will be able to keep track of the facts, figures, and work progress. You will remember better when you listen with interest. It also makes the speaker feel heard and validated, which is a great human value. Speaking takes a lot of courage; we never know the effort and practice it would have taken for a person to speak. When you listen, you indicate that their points are as valid as yours. Listening intently, nodding as a gesture to show you're engaged are some ways to make it feel like a safe space.

Your team will appreciate your openness and memory and will feel free to share their thoughts the next time, which might bring in a necessary contribution. They will feel appreciated as a consequence.

As Karl A. Menninger said, *"Listening is a magnetic and strange thing, a creative force. The friends who listen to us are the ones we move toward. When we are listened to, it creates us, makes us unfold and expand."*

Points to ponder and reflect upon

- Listening is a vital skill that should not be underestimated.
- When you listen, you open your mind to other perspectives and possibilities; you can make the people around you feel valued.
- Speak when you have to establish your position and then take the inputs from others to evaluate your position.
- Speaking is important to share your perspective and participate actively in discussions.

The group dynamics in your professional life can be crucial to how much your team can achieve. We can already see how active listening can play a vital role in group camaraderie and morale. When you listen, you show that you value their opinions and perspectives. Another crucial aspect of group dynamic, in a related vein, is when there is praise to be given around.

Even within a team project, there will be one of two people who would have contributed more to the success of a project in terms of time and enterprise. Similarly, some people would have made minor but critical contributions to the same project. Who gets the praise?

Individual credit vs. Team credit

Amar has been a first-rank student since childhood. He even topped his college and secured the best job in terms of monetary benefits.

He started working in the financial department at a large business conglomerate. His probation period of one year will be completed within a few months.

One day, Amar was getting ready to leave the office (he was looking forward to the weekend), and he spotted something on his computer. Someone in a branch office had approved a transaction for payment with a typo. The error was that an extra zero was added. Immediately, Amar flagged the transaction and called his boss. His boss, realizing the severity of the situation, called a few other senior members.

They coordinated with the team at the branch office to rectify the error. They worked over the weekend with the legal department and the supplier to get the money back. They succeeded on Monday. The CEO of the Indian operations sent a congratulatory mail thanking the finance department for spotting the error and rectifying it. The mail, however, didn't list any individual names.

What: The mail gives credit to Amar's team. However, Amar could feel that had he not spotted the error, such a ready response would not have been possible.

Who: It is clear that Amar has been a topper. He has been constantly recognized for his efforts with his academic accolades. However, his probation period at his workplace was coming to an end, and such a commendation would help him.

While he appreciated the dedication of other people who worked with him over the weekend and played equally significant roles after he identified the error, it was his diligence that caught the mistake in the first place.

Where and When: In this scenario, Amar did his job and spotted the error. It would fall within his work purview. However, he did save the company from making a humungous error. While he may not have been mentioned in the e-mail, his immediate supervisors would have noticed it.

How: Although Amar played a pivotal role, this was a team activity. While the team has been commended, Amar shouldn't go hankering for his individual credit. When the HR department schedules an interview with him at the end of the probation, he could mention it in the interview.

Why: I understand that individual recognition can be a powerful boost to one's self-esteem. However, do not let that craving make you forget the bigger picture. Whenever a team works towards a successful project, remember that teamwork is involved in its success.

Hence, on most occasions, you should err on letting the team win. Even when you feel that you may have contributed more to the project, proactively look for ways and opportunities to thank the team and appreciate every member's efforts. If you notice, whenever any sportsperson in a team sport receives an individual award, he/she will always thank their teammates and staff.

Even when actors win personal accolades, they thank the team involved in the making of the film. They recognize that the team played essential roles in their success. However, when you genuinely feel that you have led or contributed significantly in a group effort, then make sure you have taken individual credit as well. You have earned it.

It is important to have a healthy balance between the two so that you value and appreciate team efforts while making room for your individual contributions to be recognized. Everyone wants to be valued, and when you receive individual commendations, you feel that your work has been recognized and appreciated. These commendations are necessary to carve out your individual brand identity.

However, do not be in a hurry to claim the credit. When you are in a group project, your efforts should not be motivated by the need for recognition. Your motivation should be to identify where you can add value to the project and the team. It is easy to just go with the flow and do your assigned tasks.

Team credit
- Err on letting the team win.
- Proactively look for ways and opportunities to thank the team.

Individual credit
- Identify opportunities to add value.
- Take responsibility and leadership to enhance workflow.

They are safe, but they add no value to your growth, the project, or the team. So, actively look for opportunities to take responsibility and leadership to enhance the workflow. Once you spot a chance, grab it. Once you have done so and the project does well, then look to claim the credit you deserve.

You wouldn't even need to go looking for it. When you are driven by contribution and not praise, your work ethic will be contagious. People will recognize your value within the group. Thus, even if you were not to be commended in the way you wish, you will find your rightful place within the team.

Whenever you get the chance to give your team credit, do it; there is no exception to this case. Even if you feel that you contributed far more significant time and effort, give credit to your team. You can reserve a few words of credit for yourself but be generous in your praise for the team. When you do so, you foster respect and camaraderie in the team. Always praise your team publicly. This will make them feel valued and motivated to do more for the team.

Points to ponder and reflect upon

- Whenever possible, praise your team and recognize the efforts of every individual.

- Do not get motivated by the prospect of being praised. Be motivated by the need to contribute value within the workflow.
- When a project is completed successfully, you can look to claim the credit you richly deserve.

These are some of the most common tensions you are likely to face in your professional life. It doesn't matter in which stage of your career you find yourself; you will face these tensions. Always evaluate them on their individual merit. As I mentioned before, remember that there is no perfect mid-point where you can balance these tensions. Take your time and practice. Be patient about improving yourself in terms of what is right for you, along with what is right for others. Probe within yourself by reflecting on the final points, and you will find the correct balance.

3
CONTRADICTIONS IN PERSONAL LIFE

Conflicts are not solely found within our professional lives. We are bound to face tensions even within our personal lives. If you mismanage your conflicts, your relationships with others and yourself may be irrevocably harmed. These conflicts can arise from different motivations, needs, desires and values.

Our personal needs can cause a lot of friction in any relationship. We could break even the longest of our relationships when we let them stagnate without addressing the tensions.

These tensions need to be examined with understanding and compassion to find the balance. I have to stress once again that there is no static midpoint within these tensions. You need to negotiate your own personal midpoint where you can find the best balance.

In this chapter, I have identified another set of conflicts that many may commonly face in their personal lives. Each conflict will once again be introduced with a scenario and a few points to ponder upon at the end. They are:

1. Generosity vs. Saving for yourself
2. Knowing when you are right vs. Accepting learning from others
3. Agreeing vs. Disagreeing

4. Overcome anger with respect
5. Extroversion vs. Introversion
6. Material vs. Spiritual

Let us first explore the idea of being frugal or being generous. This conflict is not easy to answer as there may be many variables at play.

Balance being generous and saving for yourself

Sunil came from a family known for their contributions to society. They were never a wealthy family. However, they always extended a helping hand to people within their community. Growing up, Sunil didn't like this; he felt that his father could have brought him more toys. As years passed, Sunil entered the professional world. He was a sales executive. His first salary was due in a few days. He had looked up a few things to buy.

As he was planning this, his father came into the room. His father wanted him to allocate a small portion of his salary for charitable institutions. Sunil refused. He didn't wish to donate his hard-earned money. His father tried to explain the importance of charity, and Sunil tried to convince his father otherwise. His father realized that it was a useless conversation and decided to try again later.

Unfortunately, the next day, his father suffered a cardiac arrest. Sunil rushed him to the hospital and was surprised to see many people concerned about his father. He recognized many people as the ones his father had helped.

They had come with tokens of their love in the form of fruits, flowers and some had even collected money for his father's treatment. He was shocked and realized the value of his father's charitable work.

What: Sunil believed that his father had wasted money by being generous to other people. He thinks of it in terms of the luxuries his father had forgone for his altruistic deeds.

Who: Sunil's father knew the value of his contributions to society. He had seen people suffering and wanted to do his bit to help them out.

Where and When: As Sunil's father indicated, every religious text talks of the importance of charity. Sunil's father left no stone unturned when it came to helping people.

How: You could allocate some amount of your pay to help the society around you. However, do not make it with ulterior motives expecting something in return. Help people because you want to help them.

Why: I understand that generosity can be a virtue easily acclaimed but very challenging to put into practice. You could be facing different challenges. Some of you might be living paycheck to paycheck. You might have a mortgage to pay off. The prices of many essential goods are rising even as the income levels remain stagnant.

Your retirement fund budget is no longer the same as your parents'. You will need to save even more to survive in the future. Your children would need to be educated, and you would need to invest for a good launchpad as their parents. Where is the room to provide for others?

Being generous
- Contribute/bring your value to the community.
- Effect changes in society; learning to donate genuinely rather than for the show of it.

Saving for yourself
- Family is of primary importance.
- Maintain your backup for emergencies.

I want you to understand that generosity does not mean that you have to give away all your money. When you are in the initial stages of your career, start by donating small amounts. As you progress in your career, you could increase your contributions. Find avenues where you can donate to make a change. Your unselfish deeds would be a great character-building move. When you start contributing to society, you show that you value your community. After all, society is an important dimension in our lives. We have to value and nurture it to help it blossom.

When you are generous, you will understand the difference between a need and a want. When you see that a minuscule amount of your money can feed a hungry child, you will realize the value of your contribution. I would also encourage you to donate, not to be known for your philanthropy but for the genuine need to provide value within the community. Generally, people struggle with this dimension. Some people donate anonymously. Some people will donate and show off. Then some people don't donate at all.

If you were looking to understand which type of charity is more valuable, then it is the anonymous donation, as there is no expectation here. However, donating and proclaiming it is still better than not donating at all. On some occasions, you may need to show your donation to the wider world to highlight an issue that needs greater attention. Even if you come across people who like to talk of their charitable deeds, don't misjudge them for it. At least they are donating something to the community. If you can't afford to give money, then share your time.

Points to ponder and reflect upon

- Be generous to the extent you can contribute while being sensitive to your familial and societal requirements.
- Start with small amounts so that you can help your community grow with you.
- Err on the side of inculcating the habit to donate and contribute.

Being generous means that you recognize the difficulties of others. It strengthens our bonds with others. However, altruism isn't the only way to reach out to others. Sometimes our ego can also affect our relationships with others. When we live in a social world, there are many things we can pick up from our peers and superiors.

As we grew up, we would have received countless pieces of advice and suggestions from parents, teachers, friends and others. Kobe Bryant once said that the world is your library if you are looking to learn. We can learn a lot from the people around us. However, any human relationship is dynamic and is subject to the vagaries of the people involved. Sometimes it could be due to your own vagaries. Let's say a friend points out a problem in you. You may not like the fact that they have highlighted a flaw. You may feel slighted and would rather stick to your ground. On the other hand, your friend could have made a judgment without being privy to all the facts. Who is to blame here?

Knowing when you are right vs. Accepting learning from others:

Julia and Jenny are friends. They became roommates during their college years. They have similar likes and dislikes. They are also known for their strong opinions and the refusal to budge from them. As part of their college assignment, they had to pen down two essays. They wrote two articles filled with their firebrand opinions. When the results came out, Julia scored higher. Jenny, however, scored an average grade. Jenny contended that structurally she had got her essay spot on. She started with an argument and gave her reasons. However, she argued that she lost points because her opinion was controversial. She said that it could be that the teacher didn't agree with her opinion and thus cut the score. Julia read through Jenny's assignment and disagreed.

She pointed out her potential mistakes and where she could have tightened her opinions better. This resulted in a huge argument between the two.

What: This is a scenario where one feels that her opinion is correct and that she lost points because her opinion was controversial. She thinks that she was not evaluated based on merit.

Who: Jenny feels aggrieved that her technical skills should have scored her a better grade. She believes that the controversial nature of her opinion should not have cost her grade. Julia, meanwhile, points out where Jenny could have written better.

Where and When: Jenny perhaps needs to examine the essay once again, consider Julia's remarks, and then evaluate her essay.

How: Jenny could perhaps be down due to her average score. But maybe she should listen to Julia and find the weaknesses that were identified. She should then evaluate those points on the merit of her essay. Are her pointers valid? Could it have been written better?

Why: It is always important to be open-minded. Even the most logically strong assumptions have been challenged and rectified. In a study published in the *Science* magazine[4], it was found that only 40% of the 100 psychological experiments were found to be applicable when tested more rigorously. This brings me to the idea of intellectual humility. It is a virtue that you need to cultivate. What I mean by intellectual humility is that you need to be open to the possibility that you could be wrong. However, there is nothing wrong with being wrong. It might often come as a gift to many; as being wrong implies, you have the chance to double back, fact check, and learn more than you already know; any extra knowledge has never hurt anyone. However, it does not mean that you remain a pushover with no firm beliefs or convictions. When you feel that certain circumstances ask for your compromise regarding your values and integrity, stand strong. Provide yourself the time to find enough evidence to support what you're trying to prove.

---

[4] https://www.science.org/doi/abs/10.1126/science.aac4716

However, if your opinions are challenged, find out why they are challenged. You may feel slighted when your opinions are challenged. Hence, it is often easy to get disillusioned and feel like it is necessary to win an unsaid debate to establish some superiority.

To avoid this, pause and ponder if your time is being invested in the right place and if it is really important to voice your opinion. In many scenarios, even if the other person is supposedly wrong, they might not accept it or believe they are wrong. This could be their own internal conflict, so you must understand that you are not obligated to change their mind. This doesn't mean you must never converse with someone with a different opinion. Interact with people who hold opposing viewpoints and mutually challenge your opinions. If you only interact with people who hold similar opinions, you will become insulated in an echo chamber. This is especially true in the world of social media, where people stand firm on their opinions and do not entertain any legitimate challenge of them.

Learn from others and understand their perspectives. Try to walk in their shoes and see how they see the world. Observe their inputs, behavior and demeanor several times over. Don't just look at their perspectives from your individual contexts. Try and understand their point-of-view from a broader context as well. When you expand your scope, you will have a better idea and impression.

Think of it as how the six blind men would describe an elephant with their touch. One blind person would hold the tail, and his description would be similar to the one holding the trunk. However, this perspective will vary from the blind persons holding the tusk or touching the body. It is when you see the elephant with all its parts that you see the bigger picture. When you have this larger perspective, you will be able to confirm if your point of view is correct. If it is correct, then enforce your point of view.

A key point is that you should know when to put your foot down. People can give you feedback and advice. However, at a certain point, you should be confident about your own capabilities. There can be an endless barrage of people's commentary, feedback and criticisms.

But at a certain point, you should be able to keep faith in your inner strength and confidence. And therefore, it is important to know which key issues and challenges you will face head-on and which ones you will let go of.

Knowing when you are right

- Be confident in what you say but make sure you have checked your facts before imposing them.
- Know when to put your foot down; sometimes, you need to stand your ground.

Accepting learning from others

- Be open to different perspectives; difference in opinions doesn't mean the other is essentially wrong.
- When you are corrected, you might just learn more about it than you already know.

The tension arises when people determine that their point-of-view is correct without assessing the broader picture. When they do so, their point of view is clouded by their self-interest and is closed to other perspectives. You may have seen this behavior in prime-time partisan news debates. People only like to cast blame on others and try to assume a sense of moral superiority.

However, such behavior is a weakness. This tension can be traced to our ego. Our ego will not accept the fact that we can be wrong. We feel that any admission of error will compromise the personality that we have built. We also think that asking for help is a sign of weakness. It also does not help if you always want to win, as winning can boost your ego. It is our ego that closes our minds to the many possibilities. It will make us glean for the minutiae within instead of looking for opportunities outward. The key is to start from the other person's point of view. Observe it, try it and if it is not making sense, then stick to your own view.

Of course, when it comes to family matters, you cannot be led by the opinions of others. In times of crises, people may look to you to provide direction. Have the confidence that you can lead them out of it.

Points to ponder and reflect upon

- Recognize that we are not perfect, and we all possess our own blind spots. There is nothing wrong is admitting that you were wrong.
- There is a difference between resilience and stubbornness. It is differentiated by the willingness to learn.
- Use the perspectives of others to challenge your opinions and if they still stand firm, then hold your ground.

Intellectual humility is about learning from others and filling in your blind spots. It is about accepting the fact that you could be wrong.

However, not all personal interactions can be about learning. When you cultivate relationships with others, there will be occasions where these relationships could face friction. There will be a time when you will hold an opposing viewpoint with the other.

The other could be an acquaintance or even close family members, parents, siblings, spouse or children. It could be a difference of opinion between two partners to serious issues like buying a house or parenthood.

As I said before, we humans have our own individual needs and wants. There are bound to be occasions where these motivations could clash, causing a rift between you and your loved ones. These arguments, if left alone, could cause bigger problems. The problem we have with arguments is that we think there are only two possible choices: agree or disagree.

However, agreeing and disagreeing cannot be understood as two clear binary opposites. There can be different grades. For example, you could partially agree or strongly disagree.

There could be elements within an argument you support or a minor aspect that you find disagreeable. So how do we navigate this turbulence?

Agreeing vs. Disagreeing

Mahesh had joined a new college. He had moved to a new state. It was the first time that he had moved away from his family. He was interested in finding out what life had in store for him. He was a teetotaler. This was not because of any lack of experience. He had seen closely the negative effects of alcoholism, thanks to his neighbor. His neighbor always came home drunk and yelled at his wife and son. He had seen this disturbing behavior and was determined never to consume alcohol. Mahesh's roommates invited him to join them on their exploration of the city. On this ride, Mahesh saw his friends pull up at a bar. They claimed that it was the most happening place and that the popular kids could be found there. He joined them and ordered a glass of water. His roommates looked at him bemusedly. All of them held a beverage of their choice. They tried to get him to have a sip throughout the evening and told him he didn't know what he was missing out on. Finally, he got angry and let out a rebuke. He then got up and walked away.

What: Mahesh clearly felt uncomfortable at the pressure and had to leave. This is a case of Mahesh not succumbing to peer pressure and staying true to his values and beliefs.

Who: Mahesh is clearly motivated by his childhood experiences. He has seen the negative and detrimental effects of alcohol consumption and decided to avoid it.

Where and When: Mahesh's behavior was immaculate, considering the circumstances. He joined his friends to avoid being a social pariah. He had to finally step down in anger as he saw that his friends were not taking a clue and kept pestering him to have a sip.

How: The key here is the strength of Mahesh's convictions. He tried to negotiate and put his foot down when they weren't willing to respect his beliefs.

There is the only avenue where you cannot compromise: your beliefs. Hold on to them strongly. Disagree with anyone who doesn't respect them.

Why: One of the critical points you should remember in any disagreement is that you should be comfortable with disagreeing. Some struggle with this point as they feel compelled always to say 'yes' during discussions. There could be occasions when you think you may lose your standing with the concerned person if you disagree.

However, such behavior will turn you into a pushover. There may be some who go to the other extreme. They may argue long and hard and let the disagreement fester for a long time. When you allow conflicts to fester, they cause resentment over time – with the individual or situation.

To have a good 'disagreement' point of view, you need to have analyzed the situation carefully and then share/convince the other. Think in terms of understanding them. Do not let short tempers derail any possible conversations. Communication is key in addressing arguments of such a nature. When you are calm, you need first to ask yourself if you need to address the issue or not. If you wish to have that conversation, do not hold it to change another person's mind.

Discuss to understand their needs and perspectives. If the argument is sensitive, ask for their consent first. If you sense them to be guarded, then wait it out or move on. If they do agree to have the conversation, do so with a calm mind. However, disagreeing for the sake of it is not going to hold water. I also want you to understand that it usually takes multiple conversations to change a point of view. It cannot be changed in one go. They would have arrived at that point of view based on their experiences and thought processes.

It will take time to effect the change you wish to see, however right your opinion might be. On the flip side, don't assume that you portray a sign of weakness if you agree with an opposing view. When your perspective is challenged and changed, it displays your learning attitude. Crucially, it also shows your tolerance. It shows how you can be accepting of individuals and situations as they appear.

Disagreeing

- Stay strong to your convinctions – you need to know what you are standing for.
- To what extent can you trust someone else?

Agreeing

- Will you appear weak?
- Tolerance is a virtue (sometimes taken for granted– since you cannot proclaim it).

Points to ponder and reflect upon

- Do not look for victories in arguments.
- Try to understand the perspectives of others.
- Communication with empathy is significant in resolving arguments with loved ones.
- It is okay to have respectful disagreement positions.

I want to repeat that you should not be looking for victories in an argument. When you look for victories, you put your ego at the forefront of such a quest. When you involve your ego in arguments, you will tend to take things far more personally. So, when you feel that you are not getting the traction you desire, you may get unnecessarily offended.

It could result in the escalation of the argument and may force you down a path from which there is no return. There are countless examples of relationships that were tarnished because of such arguments.

Even the closest friends could become completely antagonistic to each other because of arguments that escalated far beyond what they should have. Such arguments can provoke feelings of hatred and dislike. Hatred is bad; it can inspire violent reactions. It shows an intractable personality that is swayed by an egoistic behavior. People may assume that hatred is the same as anger. Hatred is completely different from anger because of the context of violence. When your mind is besmirched with hatred, you will tend to look at other people as your enemies. When you feel hatred, I know it is not easy to bring back rationale to your emotions. However, you need to strive hard and rid yourself of such a potent negative emotion. One of the best ways to do this is to reflect upon your actions.

Overcome anger with respect

Matt has just moved into a new apartment complex. He happens to meet with Ben, a senior person in the same apartment. Matt likes to drink and party.

His neighbor, Ben, repeatedly knocks on his door to asks him to dial it down. This has been a constant source of irritation to Matt. Ben, however, knows that Matt is young and is full of energy. He only interrupts Matt's fun when it disturbs his sleep. Out of concern, Ben always advises Matt to control his alcohol consumption. Things got worse when Matt had a few relatives come to his place.

Ben saw him near the elevator and didn't recognize his relatives. So, he decided to advise his young neighbor again. While he didn't talk of alcohol openly, he tried to extol the virtues of self-control and austereness.

Matt was enraged. He shouted and asked Ben to shut his mouth and then angrily took his relatives to another elevator leaving behind a shocked Ben.

What: This is a scenario where an older man wants to provide good advice to his new, young neighbor. However, his advice seems like an overreaching criticism to the younger man.

Who: Matt has a perspective on life and likes to party. He sees the intervention of the elderly Ben as disapproval of himself. He dislikes that his fun gets interrupted and that he is provided with advice unasked.

Where and When: These small incidents that had remained unaddressed, has led to a sudden eruption of anger. Matt feels that Ben only likes to find faults in him.

How: Matt needs time to reflect on his behavior. He may need some distance and time to ask himself why Ben has been so persistent in his advice. Does he really have a drinking problem? These may be difficult questions to answer. However, he needs the time to cool down and probe the actual source of his frustration.

Why: There will be occasions when you burst out in anger. Venting out your frustrations is an unavoidable part of the human experience. Usually, anger surfaces when we detect a deficiency in ourselves.
So, when someone points out your faults or tells you that you can do better, it is a natural human tendency to look at such a person in an unfavorable light. There are some ways you can adopt to resolve these negative feelings. The first thing I would like to say is that there is nothing wrong with feeling upset. The first step is to extend compassion towards yourself.

It is humane to feel upset when someone hurts you. It might even be a subtle form of self-love, indicating that you deserve something more than what you have been receiving. The next step you should consider is if you want to maintain good relations with the concerned person. If you don't want to maintain the same relationship, look to set physical and emotional boundaries. Try to be civil in your future interactions.

If you treat them politely, they will reciprocate accordingly. One more crucial step would be to find your close friends and family and talk about the situation. Find the space with them to vent and grieve. Allow yourself to be heard.

Do not let it fester within you. However, if you do want to maintain the relationship, then try and communicate with them. Follow the same principles as I mentioned in the previous topic. Look for common ground and healthier ways to communicate. One way would be to look at the person and the deed differently.

Instead of seeing someone as a horrible person, think of it as someone who did an awful deed. This does not mean that I am asking you to ignore your emotions of hurt or betrayal. It is about approaching the conversation with a different mindset. There are many ways to draw boundaries respectfully. The key here is to take a moment and remember where it's coming from. They have made an effort to look out for your well-being. Even if that concern irks you at the moment, counter it with mild respect internally for the fact that they care. You may politely state that while you understand their concern, you are working on it yourself and leave the conversation at that.

You may also need to look at yourself closely. Find out why you think someone has a horrible opinion of you and what deeds or words point to such an opinion. Are there other things that could contradict such a position? It could be that one action or one conversation could cloud your entire perspective. If you did engage in a shouting match, you must follow that action of venting out with a period of calm reasoning and general calmness. Instead of wasting time on the anger after a shouting match, take your time to calm yourself and examine the situation from all angles. If you don't take the time to look at the argument with a calmer and rational mind, you may miss the point being made. You mustn't bottle your hatred within. Do not hold a grudge for too long, for you might make choices and decisions driven by this hatred. Do not let issues fester; doing so will only breed other problems, and it may steamroll into complications that may not be resolved as easily.

Regardless, it is usually not worth having burnt bridges even if you believe you would not cross on them again. In the longer run, it is probably not worth holding a grudge for too long. Losing one fight does not make you look small.

Anger
- Anger is unavoidable.
- Hatred comes because of ego – likely because one does not like being criticized.
- Be wary of decisions made in anger.

Respect
- People likely care about you.
- Bottling negative feelings will be detrimental (to you).
- Winning/losing an argument – neither is forever.

And, you have not accomplished anything just by winning one fight. These are attitudes that will affect your inner peace, along with your mental and emotional balance. Don't let your ego dictate your interactions with others.

Points to ponder and reflect upon

- Hatred leading to anger can lead to violent reactions.
- Look to set a base of civility.
- Approach your circle of friends and family to vent and grieve.
- Always look to have conversations with a calm mind.
- Examine your hatred and see if it holds weight.
- Try to understand the other party's perspective.

It is vital that you understand that your interactions and relationships with others are not a powerplay. You need to be understanding and appreciative of others and their viewpoints. It is natural that you will face points of disruption even in the most harmonious of relationships. It is up to you to be more understanding of others.

While you can extend your understanding and sympathies towards others, you also need to understand yourself. There is a reason why mental health has become a vital part of the daily discourse. One of the major psychological issues we face today is the crisis of the self. There may be many iterations of this crisis. However, common ones arise from the clash of your innate personality and the personality the world expects you to be. A quick search on the internet will lead you to 16 personalities that fall anywhere within the spectrum of introversion and extroversion. They are based on the psychological functions of Sensation, Intuition, Feeling and Thinking as identified by Carl Jung in his book, *Psychological Types*. You will find that there are different types of personalities with varying traits that can be considered extrovert and introvert. Let's discuss how to negotiate with these seemingly contrasting traits to find your own balance within this contradiction.

Introversion vs. Extroversion

Umesh was a new hire at a broadcast company. During his probation, he asked Lokesh, the highest-rated host of the company, if he could shadow him. Lokesh agreed. Lokesh was one of the most vivacious personalities he had seen. He was outgoing, and people seemed to gravitate towards him. He always had a huge smile on his face. However, there was one thing odd about Lokesh. Every day, he would take off for an hour or two and isolate himself from everyone. He would use this time for a range of activities like reading a book or meditation. Umesh could not understand the importance of this habit initially, but once he grew closer to Lokesh, he understood how necessary it was to spend time with oneself.

Lokesh needed the silence to reflect and think. He called it a 'safe place.'

What: Even though Lokesh might seem very comfortable with people around him, he needed his alone time. Lokesh practices complete silence during his alone time and uses it for personal contemplation.

Who: Lokesh is a confident person and can connect with anyone. Although he didn't know Umesh very well, he agreed to his shadowing him around. Lokesh also spends quality time with his colleagues; however, when it comes to some alone time, he makes sure to never miss out on it. He considers the time spent on personal contemplation as an important activity.

Where and When: Lokesh is an extrovert. No doubt there. However, he does shut off everyone for an hour or two every day for personal contemplation and reflection. It is up to the reader to find that balance.

How: There are no complete introverts or extroverts. We're all ambiverts; we fall in different spaces within that spectrum.
While you need to spend time with others for feedback and criticism, you need some along time to reflect, reinforce your values and remind yourself of your goals and motivations. You must find the right balance between both these extremes.

Why: Do not worry if you find yourself leaning more towards being an introvert or an extrovert. There is nothing like one right personality. If you are an introvert, try to spend some time with others and encourage yourself to get comfortable with them. If you are uncomfortable, then start small. Try interacting within your group first, and then work your way up to a different crowd.

If you are an extrovert, then embrace your personality. However, do not go overboard in your search for stimulation. Fix a time within your calendar where you can be social.

Find people with like-minded interests. For example, if you are a fitness enthusiast, you could join a gym or a running group. It will help refine your interests. You will improve and discover new aspects of yourself.

However, it is also vital that you take some time for yourself to reflect on your actions and accomplishments. Try to analyze them and learn from what may have worked and what may have not. Solitude is highly recommended to realize your identity.

The world is always changing, and we are not different. We are not the people we were yesterday, so you must spend time with the person you are evolving into. Who you are comes from within, no matter who you spend time with or what you do. They can only inspire you and motivate you. Only you can work on your identity.

Do not get too comfortable within these personalities. Challenge yourself to go outside of your comfort zone once in a while. You need such challenges to grow even if they make you uncomfortable. Challenging yourself will help you get flexible and act according to the situation you are in.

If you are in a leader's position, you will find people with a mix of these personalities. It is crucial that you educate yourself on these personalities and bring the best out of them. You would need constant interactions. You need to encourage the introverts to speak up and the extroverts to listen.

Extroversion
- Externally seen to be bold and open to stepping out of the comfort zone.
- Open to be broadly surrounded with people – broadly energies flowing from outside-in.

Introversion
- Inclined to be self-dependent.
- Enjoy your solitude – with energies flowing inside out.

Points to ponder and reflect upon

- There are no absolute extroverts or introverts.
- Find your traits that you can enhance and work on.
- Introverts must embrace their personalities and challenge themselves to get out of their comfort zones once in a while. On the other hand, extroverts must utilize the opportunity and look within.

There is nothing wrong with being an introvert or an extrovert. The problem is when you mistakenly associate the idea of one personality being better than the other.

Remember, you are unique and have something to offer to the world. Embrace yourself and find the strengths within you. Everyone has some personality traits that make them special. Identify your traits and work on them. Challenge yourself, and you will be able to shed the carapace of any negativity around yourself.

All that being said, it is also vital to be in touch with your spiritual self. When you lose touch with the spiritual facet of your life, you will find yourself far more dissatisfied. You cannot lead a spiritual life when you lead a worldly life. However, you can always lead a spiritual life when you are fulfilling your material needs.

Balancing the material and spiritual self:

Ron has been inclined towards spirituality since childhood. He visited the church every Sunday as a kid. However, things changed. He had to cut down on his visits to the church once he took up a job; his job involved a lot of traveling.

Ron's job paid well, and he could afford a mortgage on a nice house that he and his wife picked out. However, the pressure soon started to crush Ron. The constant work and family pressure made him feel out of place.

Things got worse as Ron was just not able to visit the church. To help him, his wife presented him with a rosary gifted by the pastor of his church. This rosary would become a source of solace for Ron.

Whenever he was in a tough spot, Ron would just hold the rosary and pray to God. He would immediately feel all the tensions melting away.

What: Ron experiences the pressures of the material world. His mortgage and increased bills, and the nature of his job has worn him down. However, it is his failure to pray at the church that has left him the weariest.

Who: Ron, being a spiritual person, feels torn by the fact that the pursuit of material benefits has led him astray from God's flock.

Where and When: It is the rosary that gives Ron perspective. You don't have to go to a regulated center of worship to pray and thank the Lord. You need to keep a personal connection with God to experience his blessings. Even if you are an atheist or agnostic, it is about leading an honest life with humility and gratitude.

How: Think of it as a penance. If you think of the Hindu scriptures and tales, God only appears in front of those, be it the virtuous or the devious, who have done their penance. It requires perseverance. The idea is that you lead an honest life filled with goodness, compassion, empathy and humility.

Why: An issue arises when we think of spiritual life in terms of renunciation, suffering and penance. These are extreme ideas that we should look to moderate when we look to balance our material life and spiritual life. There is nothing wrong with trying to earn money. The problem lies when we make it the sole focus of our living. Material benefits must be the focus of our livelihood and not our life. I will turn to the *Bhagawad Gita* to provide an answer.

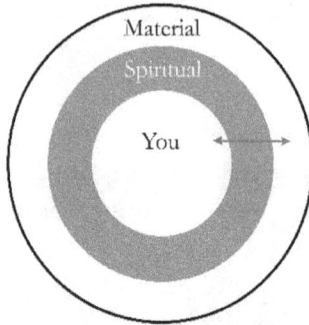

Balance of the material and spiritual

The Gita talks of how we can make our activities God-centric for balancing the material requirements of life with the spiritual attainments we need. So, if we were to look at earning money to sustain our families and their needs, we are doing our spiritual duty to look after our families. The idea lies not in individual fulfillment but in fulfilling social responsibilities. You have to find the spiritual meaning behind your daily material activities. When you look to earn money, you do it as your dharma to your family. You are playing the role of a provider as your spiritual duty.

Material
- Material comforts can lead to a comfortable life.
- Bills and payments need to be made.

Spiritual
- On the path to self-realization.
- Inculcates a sense of gratitude for the life lived.

Other ways we could look to balance both these lives would be to follow what Ron did.

We could chant the name of God regularly while doing other chores. Regular prayer is another alternative. Offer your prayers to God and thank him for the fortune He has bestowed upon you.

That gratitude will give you the detachment you need from the material pleasures as you recognize His blessings. Another alternative would be to read spiritual texts regularly.

When we read spiritual texts, we inculcate a spiritual discipline. If you do not believe in the existence of God, then balance your material joys with silent moments of gratitude for a good life. It is important to temper your enjoyment with this balance as material gains are transient. What you may possess today may be lost tomorrow.

"*Sound mind in a sound body*" is a famous quote by the pre-Socratic Greek philosopher Thales. It demonstrates the close connection between physical exercise, mental stability, and the ability to enjoy one's life. Hence, balancing material possessions and spirituality is a concept that needs to be studied and pondered upon in-depth. This balance can be read adjacent to the balance we discussed when we explored the contradiction between being content and ambitious.

When you negotiate your life's material gains and accomplishments, you cannot be inflated with a sense of pride. This balance is about becoming comfortable with your achievements, wherein you are not swayed by your successes or failures.

It is about leading an honest life, untainted by hubris even when no one is looking.

Points to ponder and reflect upon

- It is entirely possible to lead a life which is balanced between material requirements and spiritual attainments.
- Do not look for individual fulfillment when you pursue material benefits; instead think of social responsibilities like taking care of your family and your contributions to society.
- Balance your material pursuits with spiritual activities like praying, chanting God's name, and reading spiritual texts.

These activities will help you stay grounded. It will also help you be thankful for the blessings bestowed on you. These practices are another way to keep your ego in check!

- Lead an honest life, even when no-one is looking.

These are some of the tensions in your personal life that need reflection. Take your time to assess where you stand when it comes to your relationships with others. As a thumb rule, always evaluate your personal experiences with a calmer mind. Do not let your emotions run roughshod as they are more liable to creating further complications.

Remember, complications aren't a full stop. It is a chance for you to pause and reflect on what is right and how you want to move further. In fact, it is because of these complications that you know what exists on both sides and what you must choose to lead a balanced life.

4

BALANCING PERSONAL AND PROFESSIONAL CONTRADICTIONS

We have explored the potential conflict zones in our professional and personal lives. However, there are a set of tensions that will not be exclusive to either professional or personal lives. In this chapter, I intend to examine a few contradictions that can impact you professionally and personally. They are:

1. Work vs. Family
2. Balance in relationships
3. Balancing interactions with people
4. Dreaming vs. Living in reality
5. Patience vs. Urgency

The most discussed idea of work-life balance can be traced to the idea of balancing work time and family time. This is a challenge, especially in a world where both partners are working. We often find ourselves in misunderstandings and, consequently, dissatisfaction. This tends to happen in relationships when there is a lack of communication between the two parties, which is a very common picture in modern families. So how should we navigate through this to find the perfect balance? Let's find out.

Balancing family and work

Vince was an enterprising young man. He came from a family with minimum means. He was determined not to be trapped in similar circumstances. He studied hard until he finished his GED. He then realized that he couldn't afford college and the debt he would accumulate.

So, he decided to work during the day and enroll in an evening community college course. It was at this time he met Rachel. Rachel was a beautiful woman, and she too came from a family of minimum means. They fell in love and got married. Vince was determined to take care of Rachel and present her with everything she desired. He took up more part-time jobs to increase the wealth of the family. In just a few months, the couple was expecting.

Now, Vince had to take up more jobs to provide for his family. He doubled down on his work as he didn't want his children to experience what he went through as a kid. He rarely had any time for his family.

He didn't even find the time to share a meal. When it was pointed out to him, he said that he needed to work harder, and once he succeeded, he would have the time to spend with them. He soon graduated and got a better-paying job. He was able to move to a better part of the town. It was at this point that Rachel was expecting again.

Vince then thought that he needed to work harder as it was one more extra mouth to feed. So, he started working overtime and once again didn't have the time to spare for his family. His work ethic was recognized, and he was swiftly promoted.

Over the years, he swiftly moved up the ladder. Unfortunately, his responsibilities only grew with time, and he could not spend any quality time with his family. He moved his family to a luxurious house and employed maids to make their lives comfortable. It was one of those days that Vince returned exhausted. His family was already asleep. He closed his eyes out of exhaustion and didn't open them again.

What: This is a classic scenario of Vince pushing himself beyond his limits to provide for his family. He worked so hard that he worked himself to death all alone. His family was already used to Vince being absent; however, now, they had to live without him forever.

Who: Vince is a classic example of a person who forgot for whom he was working. He wanted to work tirelessly for the good of his family. However, he never got the time to enjoy any of it with his family.

Where and When: Vince should have made the time to spend quality time with his family. He could have taken a few vacations. Perhaps his family could have done with a little less of the wealth and a lot more of his health.

How: Vince needed to get some perspective. He should have planned his time better. Instead of just focusing on work, Vince should have spent more time with his children. He should have allocated time to enjoy the fruits of his labor with his family.

Why: When we work, we tend to forget why we put in those efforts. So, let us first examine the possible motivations for your diligent efforts in the professional sphere. You could work hard to lead a comfortable life with your family. You want to ensure that there is never a lack of anything for your family's needs. Every action would derive from the fundamental fact that you work to better your family and yourself. It is when people forget this fact that they put the family on the backburner. You must find the time for your family.

I came across this quote by Gary Keller, the real estate entrepreneur: "*Work is a rubber ball. If you drop it, it will bounce back. The other four balls – family, health, friends, and integrity – are made of glass. If you drop one of those, it will be irrevocably scuffed, nicked, perhaps even shattered.*" Don't ever discount the importance of your family. It is your circle of trust where you can share your burdens freely without fear of judgment.

If you lose or shatter your family to pursue professional excellence, you will never cherish the professional rewards the same.

So, how can you find time for family when you are stuck in the rat race? The answer lies in planning your calendar. I have to emphasize the importance of planning and scheduling your life better.

Begin by marking important days for your family and organize your life around these days. These dates could be anniversary dates, birthdays and dates of remembrance.

When you schedule your calendar thus, you will find that you can balance your work and family time better. One quote that I found relevant here is that from Stephen Covey. He said, *"The key is not to prioritize what's on your schedule, but to schedule your priorities."*

So, ensure that your family is your first priority and not your work. It is vital that you also schedule some time for fun. This does not mean that you plan for many fun days and ignore your responsibilities at work. Work hard and find something fun to do after your work. When you schedule something fun after your work, there will be a sense of anticipation even as you work.

Work is not an end goal in life

"Never get so busy making a living that you forget to make a life." – Dolly Parton

One of the biggest blunders you might commit is to turn to your job for the fulfillment in your life. This statement is not meant to discount any professional success but rather to highlight how narrow-minded such an approach can be.

When you put your job at the center of your life, you only set your professional career prospects as the end goal. Such an end goal sacrifices many other valued facets of your life. It would be ideal to look at your life in terms of these four dimensions:

Family, Personal, Professional/Work, Society

When you schedule your life around all these facets, you will lead a much happier and well-balanced life. Each of these dimensions demands great energy and commitment. So, you cannot discount the importance of any of these four dimensions. You will have to push and pull and budget for all these dimensions when it comes to your time. You have to find the balance between all these four dimensions.

For example, let us say you are a CEO and call yourself a rockstar CEO. You cannot claim to be a rockstar CEO when you fail on the personal and family fronts. You may argue that your handsome pay packet as the CEO will provide your family with all material luxuries. However, it is not enough to provide only material comforts. You also need to give them your time. This is especially true during the formative years of your children. Author Regina Brett's quote will help you put this in perspective: *"Your children get only one childhood. Make it memorable."*

So, you need to interact and engage with your family constantly. Ask them about their interests and ambitions. Partake in those activities and enjoy your time with them. Let them know that you care. Your family can also be a good sounding board. They can help you see things from a new perspective. When you show that you care for their interests and aspirations, they will reciprocate the same care to your interests and goals. For instance, I am writing this book with the push from my wife as a collection of vital thoughts I want to impart to our son.

I, too, had to let go of the cycle when I saw my son cycle for the first time without the training wheels. His first ride was exhilarating, and I remember his joy. I want him to experience life in that same rapture and not lose balance whenever he experiences these tensions. From my personal experience, I've had many a great success on the professional front, but the best memories are all private moments shared with my family and friends.

It would be best if you remember that your professional success is relatively short-lived. There will always be a new peak to scale, and it will come with greater expectations attached.

However, what will remain with you is your family's support, love, affection and generosity.

Work
- Considerable boost to self-worth.
- Several comforts for the family require capital investment.

Family
- Prioritize your time with family over the money spent on them.
- Family is a great sounding board – choices made as a team.
- You work for the betterment of your family and yourself; never forget that priority.

You may be confused by the two separate dimensions of Personal and Family. You may think that these are interchangeable. They are not. I want to stress that your personal goals and interests are also vital.

You need to give time for your own interests and hobbies. Never let others dictate it. It may even be hard to discover something you feel truly passionate about.

Feel free to explore as many fields as you can before you settle. Your hobbies and interests are important. They might make an unexpected contribution to your work life; you never know.

There is always something to learn that you can apply in multiple stages of your life. For example, creating art might not look like it can contribute to your work or personal life balance, but it teaches you a lot about trusting the process, being patient, and the essence of observation. Likewise, any interest of yours will contribute on a larger scale if you spend a bit of time polishing and honing it.

Carl Sandburg, the poet, said, *"Time is the coin of your life. It is the only coin you have, and only you can determine how it will be spent. Be careful lest you let other people spend it for you."*

Make the time for your own development. It could be activities like regular exercise, runs, grooming and golf. Indulge in things you like along with what your family enjoys as well. If you are happy, your family will be happy, and consequently, your professional world will also be happy. They are all inter-connected in a loop.

Finally, let us talk about your potential contribution to society, i.e., the people around you. You should actively think about engagement and contribution to society. Contribute your wealth, time, and talent, which is described as the 3 Ts: Time, Treasure and Talent in the Rotary world. Try and engage with local charities and do some work to uplift your community. Do your bit and do it to the extent you can. Remember what we have discussed in the previous chapters, while being generous is a vital trait, always prioritize what is essential. It means to focus on what needs the most attention from you in that moment and scheduling accordingly; the tasks should not seem overwhelming to you.

When you start leading a well-rounded life by balancing all these dimensions, you will soon find that somewhat oddly, your family and your surroundings replicate and follow your mantra. So, plan your schedule around these four dimensions. However, you cannot design it as 25% of the week for each dimension—plan according to the circumstances. However, I would also caution you from packing your calendar to the brim when you cater to all these dimensions. If you fill your calendar completely, you would be living your life at full pelt. Rather, you will be living life at 120%. I would recommend that you keep yourself occupied for 90% of the day.

Keep the rest of the time to rest and let your mind reflect. Only when you allocate some time for thought and reflection will you find that your mind becomes a fertile ground for new ideas and fresh perspectives. You may have heard of people who come across brilliant ideas when they are alone. Those ideas come during that time because that is the only time their mind is stress-free. When you find yourself with new ideas and fresh perspectives, you will find that you will be able to reinforce, review, revise and refine your current work.

You will be able to simplify complex issues and optimize your work. It may not seem true; however, when you make time for your personal and family's interests and happiness, your professional life too will bear the fruits of that enjoyment. Remember that your greatest personal asset is time, which you must choose to invest wisely.

These words I read have stuck with me for a long time: "*Most of us, care for things (material gains) and Use people. But for a happy life, it is the other way around, care for people and use things.*" If you have your balance right, you will find ways to put your family and yourself first and work in the right perspective.

But Work is Also Critically Important

As I stress the importance of making time for all the other dimensions, do not assume that I am placing work in the backseat.

Making time for yourself does not mean you compromise on your professional life. It is equally as important as your personal and family time. Only when you work well will you get the capital to enjoy your time with your family. Some people will have had the privilege to work hard in a role they are incredibly passionate about. If you are one of them, do remember why you started on this path. It is entirely valid for your job to be just about capital, but it is just as valid if you are doing it for the sake of your passion.

Set milestones for yourself to achieve and strive to complete them. Try to enjoy this process rather than setting your mind entirely on accomplishments. Your professional success may be fleeting, but they do provide a considerable boost to your self-worth. It is a vital part of your individual sense of accomplishment. I'm sure you would have been proud and felt at the top of the world whenever you succeeded in any professional task. There will be cycles of work where you need to peak and balance your family life.

But do not compromise on the personal front when it comes to grooming and your physical fitness. Staying healthy is the first order of business.

It is so easy to get blindsided by the fast-moving world that we tend to forget that our body is working tirelessly every day to keep us alive. It is almost disrespectful not to return the favor. Only when you are healthy can you spend time on all the dimensions of your life.

Points to ponder and reflect upon

- You work for the betterment of your family and yourself; never forget that priority.
- Plan your calendar to find the apt work-life balance.
- Plan your calendar around five dimensions: Work, Family, Personal, Society and Rest.

It is vital that you schedule your calendar properly. Balancing your work and family is one of the most common issues people face. However, when we speak of family, we need to talk about relationships. You may find that maintaining good relationships require commitment and patience. As we covered in the previous chapter, all it needs is one wrong conversation to damage years' worth of relationships. While we discussed how we could negotiate our interactions, I would like to explore relationships and the problems they could face.

Now there are two distinct types of relationships: personal and professional. A personal relationship will be built on mutual trust and friendship. It will have greater depth and warmth. A professional relationship will be built on mutual interests. It will be more transactional and will lack the same intimacy as a personal relationship. However, it is always possible that both relationships could end up being the other as well. A close professional relationship could lead to a good personal relationship and vice-versa.

However, no matter the type of relationship, they are incredibly tough to manage. You need to be there in the moment, especially during tough times, to help navigate troubled waters.

Balance in relationships

Tejas and Rohini worked in two competing companies. They are also happily married. Tejas currently finds himself in trouble. His work has always been exemplary. He was constantly commended for his efforts. However, Tejas ruined a meeting with an important client and lost the deal. In a cruel twist of fate, it was Rohini who landed the deal for her company. Tejas was publicly reprimanded in his company. This dressing down embarrassed Tejas, which bled into his personal life and soured his relationship with his wife.

Tejas became irritable with his wife, which led to her reciprocation in kind. Soon, they started to snap at the smallest tick leading up to the filing of a divorce. When the court ordered them to counseling, they went in looking to salvage the relationship. It was here that they started speaking honestly with each other. They bared the hurts they had inflicted on each other and began the journey to save their relationship.

What: This is a case of how communication is important for the blossoming of a relationship. They let the issues fester to the point that they had to go to court for divorce proceedings. Because they let the issues fester, there was much hurt to sift through to heal their relationship.

Who: Tejas might have felt slighted when his wife snapped a deal that he botched. The personal nature of the failure could have dealt him a severe blow. It is clear that his exemplary work and commendations have been an avenue for his self-esteem. However, when he failed, his wife became the source of his discontent.

Where and When: They should have had an open and honest conversation on the same day he was reprimanded publicly.

How: There was clear friction between the couple. They should have taken the time to look at the situation from each other's shoes.

Tejas had been humiliated, and his ego was hurt. On the other hand, Rohini didn't want to be facing the brunt of her husband's ire. If they had talked and reminded themselves that they loved each other, they would not have hurt each other more.

Why: Love and affection will let you overcome a lot of differences in opinion. When you care and love someone, it will help you look past the deficiencies and shortcomings. The other person could be anyone; it could be your spouse, your child or your sibling.

"Too often we underestimate the power of a touch, a smile, a kind word, a listening ear, an honest compliment or the smallest act of caring, all of which have the potential to turn a life around." – Leo Buscaglia

Your care and concern, which arises from your love and affection, can be like a salve for the wounds and cuts of the human experience. It could be the grease that helps smoothen rickety and rusty cogs and wheels to make a machine run smoothly. Failures, mistakes, hurt and pain are unavoidable parts of human life. These failures or mistakes will cause many problems. The love and affection shown by a person's near and dear ones will alleviate some of the burdens. Without the grease of love and empathy, friction is inevitable, leading to greater wounds and pain.

One side
- Be generous in your benefit of doubt.
- Genuine concern and care will let you overcome a lot of differences in opinion, while being accommodative.

Other side
- Ease your own stress by being consciously less judgmental.
- Empathy in relationships is needed for it to operate smoothly.

If you truly love someone, be patient and understanding. However, this does not mean that you are not entitled to your opinion. If you feel some occasion needs you to stand up, then stand your ground. The ideal way to live in a relationship is to balance living with your heart and brain. You cannot force cold logic on every situation. Some situations may ask for the warmth of a hug and understanding. One key element to remember is that if you want relationships to thrive, never bottle your frustrations. Don't let it fester into grudges. Sometimes you will need to forgive, forget and move on. One key thing to remember is that it takes more than just love to maintain a healthy relationship. It also requires honesty and patience. The first sign of a healthy relationship is the open lines of communication. Both parties are not afraid to share, and it never feels one-sided.

The second sign of a healthy relationship is that they accept disagreements. A healthy relationship isn't one where one person's likes and dislikes become the norm. Instead, they would be willing to disagree and recognize that they can actually use the conflict to share their unique perspectives. The key in their disagreement is that they disagree over some issue and not the person.

Another sign of a healthy relationship is that people in the relationships maintain their own unique individual identity. They are not afraid to share their quirks in fear of judgment. They would also maintain a strong sense of their selves outside their relationship. However, they are very considerate of the other whenever they make any decisions.

Points to ponder and reflect upon

- Love and affection will help smooth over issues in any relationship.
- A relationship is a human exercise and function, and forcing cold logic on it may prove detrimental.
- Honesty and patience are a must for maintaining a healthy relationship.

It is clear that we need to be honest and patient in our relationships with others. One of the critical components in a healthy relationship is the openness of the interactions. In the previous chapter, we discussed how we could negotiate with disagreements and the possible consequences.

However, how can you minimize the possible misunderstandings? How should you behave to ensure a smooth and harmonious relationship? How would you act in the company of peers or the company of seniors or juniors? Would you look to be a chameleon and change your colors based on the company? Do you depend on others to validate yourself? These are some of the questions you need to confront when you probe into your relationships with others. Remember to maintain your honesty and individuality within any interactions, no matter who the other person is.

Balancing interactions with people

Rahul and Raj were childhood friends. They went to the same school and later to the same college. Their parents fostered a sense of competition between the two; it started with the grades at school. Raj was slightly better when it came to academics. Raj was also excellent in sports. People considered Raj as the more well-rounded individual of the two. While Raj was his friend, Rahul was certainly miffed with the perception that Raj's excellence in sports made him a more well-rounded person.

After their college graduation, Rahul took up a job with the best pay package. However, this meant that his work hours were longer. Raj took a job in a different state. His job didn't pay as much, but he took the job nevertheless. Rahul was surprised. Raj was offered a job at the same company and the same level as Rahul. Rahul couldn't fathom why Raj didn't take the job. Upon asking, he learned that Raj wanted to be away from Rahul. He remarked that Rahul had started being a bit snappy and snarky with him for no fault of his own from a certain point in high school.

Raj felt that Rahul was no longer the fun guy he knew. He brooded whenever Raj scored higher on a paper and made remarks that subtly undermined Raj's efforts. Raj was done with that kind of treatment.

What: This is a scenario where a long-term friendship broke down because of the lack of honest conversation. Both felt wronged for one situation or the other. They started as healthy rivals, and soon that desire for winning eroded the depth of their relationship.

Who: Rahul, on reflection, realized that he was misled, all thanks to other's remarks and opinions. People speculated that his friend Raj was better; Rahul was stuck with feelings of jealousy and inadequacy. Rahul never realized this and ended up passing comments that undermined Raj's achievements. On the other hand, Raj decided to withdraw because the best option, according to him, was to move to a new place.

Where and When: At a certain point, Rahul had to reflect on his comments and his relationship with Raj. Raj, on the other hand, should have tried to nip it in the bud. He should have brought the issue to Rahul's attention earlier. If he had addressed the problem earlier, they could have buried the hatchet and healed their relationship.

How: It could have been done with an open and honest conversation. Maybe Rahul would have realized his fears of inadequacy and worked on them.

Why: It can be challenging not to be swayed by the opinion of others. There is always a part within that seeks a second opinion or validation from others. However, this can affect your inner balance. Your external interactions with other people will have an impact on you. You will come across people whose motivations might be antagonistic to your aims. They may even cross a line.

However, don't judge people (and definitely don't judge them based on a few actions). It would be best to remember that no one is entirely good or bad. When you come across people who may seem antagonistic to you, don't let that initial perspective cloud their good deeds. You will experience friction and disagreements even with the people closest to you. When there are contrasting aims and interests, someone will inevitably have to give way and get hurt. The key is not to let that dictate your future interactions.

"If you have an ongoing relationship with a person, think of everything positive about that person that you possibly can and enter your interaction from that space. Ignore all the crap that used to drive you up the wall before. You will be amazed at what a change this attitude shift brings about."
— Srikumar Rao

One side
- Peer pressure – understand that there is more to life than one set of individual comparisons!
- People are never entirely good or bad – there are circumstances and shades of all in all.
- Forget/forgive for the most part.

Other side
- Strive to broaden your perspectives.
- Engage your heart and brain in people interactions.
- Push your efforts with those stronger than you, while being gentle with those weaker.

Sometimes people close to you may end up being bad, inadvertently. They may not realize that their actions might be causing harm or hurting you. And the same person may be good in a different context or a different interaction. So, you have to balance that good with the mean side. When you do so, you will find a difference in your interactions with others. You will find that arguments won't weaken the strength and depth of your relationship.

"I feel very lucky to have grown up having interactions with adults who were making change but who were far from perfect beings. That feeling of not being paralysed by your incredible inadequacy as a human being, which I feel every day, is a part of the legacy that I've gotten from so many of the adult elders." –
Marian Wright Edelman

Broaden the lens you are viewing people with

There are a few interactions that you need to examine from a broader perspective:

Competing and peer pressure: I'm sure competition has been a part of your childhood. It could have started from the playground boasts as children of how awesome your parents are. It could have expanded then to grades and games on the ground. One thing to note is that healthy competition between peers is a good thing.

It pushes you to reach beyond your limits. It will show you that your potential can be greater. However, the key operative word is healthy competition. This leads to the question; how can you ensure that you keep competition healthy? To ensure that your competition is healthy, it would be best not to think of it as just a win-loss record. Think of it as a process to grow and evolve. When you hold such a mentality, you will be able to celebrate the successes of others in letter and spirit.

When you are gracious in your losses, you will ensure that negative emotions of envy or anger do not hinder your growth. I have always preferred to chart a course that made the most sense to me in my life. But I've seen many who react to competition or want to compete with others. They thrive in the challenge and do better than what we assume. When you compete, balance it with the view that the world is much bigger than just any one individual. It would help to remember that you are not the center of the world. Kobe Bryant, who was known for his fierce competitive drive, spoke of failure. He said that whenever he worried that his failure and mistakes would be magnified in the media, he used to tell himself only one thing. He would say to himself, get over yourself.

He used to remind himself that he was not that important. Then he would examine his failure and look to address it in his practice and training. It will be ideal to remember that there is much more to life than the competition, regardless of who wins or loses. This broader perspective is so important for you to stay grounded as you progress in life.

Managing people: When you manage people in the office, be nice and kind to them. You should also be stern with them. I've found that you need to build your life rock-solid in a few areas (including your principles and values). And, in some other areas, you must be flexible. Building this right balance is the key to managing people in the workplace. You should be very firm on your principles and positions. Never compromise on them. However, always ensure that you are open to being flexible and receptive to other perspectives. Your character, honesty, diligence should be non-negotiable, but you must be willing to understand the challenges your staff might be dealing with. In other words, this situation is similar to managing a young kid.

There will be areas where you let the kid be a kid; you let them learn from their mistakes. However, when it comes to certain other areas, you will not let them be free. If they are not allowed to go near the fireplace, they should obey your orders and stay put. In scenarios like these, you must put your foot down and discipline them. Managing people is definitely an art that is learned.

Differences of opinion: When you find yourself in an argument (best is to not land in one in the first place!), you will find that you are deaf to the point of view of the other aggrieved party. You may tend to think that your argument is infallible and is grounded in reason and logic. However, to be truly balanced, you will take the time to understand the perspective of the other party and appreciate their stance. I'm not saying that you must renounce your position. However, you must learn to appreciate the opposite party's viewpoint.

When you understand the other view, you will come to a logical conclusion instead of a heated end. You may discover that it is not a zero-sum game and that both point-of-views can co-exist and find their acceptance. When you look to understand the viewpoints of others, people will find their interactions with you to be useful, and they will take the time to understand your perspective. You will also learn to accept people despite their differences. This is especially important for people in leadership positions. Your compassion and empathy will endear you to people more.

You will also find that you will be less prone to fall to potential prejudices. In fact, you will be less judgmental of people and build a wonderful balance in your interactions with people. When you work, there is a thumb rule that you can follow.

Fight and push for opportunities with people who are above you in the hierarchy. However, when you deal with people who report to you, be kind to them.

Points to ponder and reflect upon

- Do not seek external validation; look inwards and validate yourself—this is a strong sign of your self-confidence.
- Do not let one antagonistic action cloud your perception of the other person.
- A healthy competition with your peers will help you grow; do not focus on a win-loss record.
- Be firm in your values and principles. But also, try to understand the other person's point of view.
- Fight and push for opportunities with people above you in the flow of command and be kind to the people below you in the same flow of command.

When it comes to relationships, it is ideal to be understanding. However, do not compromise on your own self-worth to be understanding of others.

You have to stand up for yourself as the chances are that no one else will. One of the biggest mistakes you can make is to look for validation from others. You must provide that to yourself. It might not be easy to start validating yourself. Sometimes the very reason for seeking external validation might be the harsh criticism received at some point of our lives. But you must understand, needing validation from others is an expectation you place on them, and such expectations are usually let down.

This is not to say that you must never expect to receive appreciation in your professional/personal relationships but to say you must not let somebody else's validation determine your worth. One of the best ways to boost your self-worth and self-esteem is by setting goals and achieving them.

You need to have a dream and work towards achieving that dream. There are two things that we do with our dreams. Either we draw up a plan and work towards achieving them or discard them and regret not taking a chance.

However, chasing your dreams requires more than just your resolve. Commitment and perseverance are a must to accomplish your goals.

Balancing dreaming and living in reality

Alex and Brad wanted to be great football players. They both practiced hard and worked their way up in the youth levels. Brad was hardworking, and he worked tirelessly. Alex, who was widely recognized to be the better talent, found something fun to do.

Both of them had gained a level of fame for their prodigious talent. Alex saw this as an opportunity to bask in his newfound fame. He started cutting down on his practice and started wasting time in other fruitless ventures.

Ten years later, Alex was sitting in a restaurant when he saw a football match being shown on the TV. His old friend, Brad, was captaining the national team in the World Cup. He could only sigh in regret as he thought he, too, could have been part of the team.

After a few minutes, he could only point to Brad and tell the fellow patrons that he and Brad used to be childhood friends and played together in the same team.

He also couldn't help but tell people that he was considered a better talent. The fellow patrons smiled at him bemusedly and went on their way, leaving Alex to reflect on the what-ifs of life.

What: This is a classic scenario of what-ifs. What if Alex had put in the same effort in his training as Brad? What if he didn't fall into the trappings of fame? What if he hadn't wasted his prime on fruitless ventures?

Who: Alex is left with a lot of regrets as he lost track of his dreams. He gave up the work and dedication needed to achieve his goal. He got entrapped by the many distractions of fame.

Where and When: Alex should have taken time to reflect on his actions. He should have seen the work of Brad and realized that he wasn't putting in the same effort. Had he looked at his situation carefully, the results would have been different.

How: If Alex had taken the time to reflect, he would have reconnected with his dream and found the energy to resume his work and accomplish his goals.

Why: I'm sure many of you had dreams you wanted to achieve. If, by any reason, you have been restricting yourself of that joy, please retreat and let yourself dream. However, having a dream is not enough. It demands your commitment and passion.

Say you wanted to get into one of the top colleges in the world. You cannot just wish it into reality. These institutions demand a certain level of academic excellence. You will have to put in the effort to ensure that you are strong academically and fulfill the criteria needed. Some of these colleges may also give you bonus points for related extra-curricular activities.

So, you will need to hone your craft in these activities to separate yourself from the pack.

"Do not wait; the time will never be just right. Start where you stand, and work with whatever tools you may have at your command, and better tools will be found as you go along." – George Herbert

Dreaming
- Expand your ambition with a desire to achieve.
- Chart your course into the future.

Living in reality
- Translate the 'realistic' dreams into a series of actions/tasks/plans that you need to take.
- Procrastination will not get you far.

While it is important to dream, you cannot be stuck in the dreaming phase. By wasting time, you are just going far away from your goals. Similarly, you cannot be just stuck at crossing things from a to-do list. You will then just be a slave to routine. You need to reconnect with your dreams to remind yourself of why you are putting in the effort.

As Pauline Kael said, *"Where there is a will, there is a way. If there is a chance in a million that you can do something, anything, to keep what you want from ending, do it. Pry the door open or, if need be, wedge your foot in that door and keep it open."*

You get the drive and courage to keep the door open when you are in touch with your passion and dreams. So, when you do knock off tasks to achieve your goals, take moments to enjoy your accomplishments, however minor or major they seem.

When you dream and think about it, there is a good chance that your mind will chart a course to see it through action. However, there is a tendency to procrastinate. Such habits will only deter you. You need to act immediately and work towards your goals.

Understand that your actions and habits have consequences. When you procrastinate, you are sending a subconscious signal to yourself that your goal is not that important. It may deviate you from your purpose in the long run. There may be many reasons behind your procrastination.

You must sit on it for a moment and examine what's stopping you from doing your work. Many times, it may be the fear of failure. It is natural to be afraid before taking the big leap, but you mustn't let your fear stop you.

Failure is not your end game. In fact, failure may even be a necessity to learn better. As clichéd as this saying sounds, you learn from your mistakes. So, allow yourself to try before assuming the worst-case scenario. It is crucial that you translate your dream into a set of targets and actions.

You need to work towards it. When you work towards your goal and keep in touch with your dreams, you will find immense satisfaction from every successful completion of a task towards that goal.

"Don't watch the clock; do what it does. Keep going." – Sam Levenson

Points to ponder and reflect upon

- Dreams are important to let your ambitions soar and fly. They will open the door to a world full of possibilities.
- You cannot wish a dream into reality.
- It requires passion, commitment, and perseverance to accomplish your dreams.
- Don't get stuck dreaming, and don't get stuck completing your tasks like a to-do list. Keep in touch with your dreams and celebrate your achievements on the way.

When you work towards achieving your goals, you are bound to come across many opportunities that may seem tempting. They will feel especially attractive in a world that is driven by the fear of missing out. We live in a world driven by trends and bandwagons.

Many people may come to you promising you quick routes to success. The real attraction to the scheme could be its temporality. The key is to evaluate it before blindly leaping into it. We have already covered the idea of patience and persistence when it comes to your professional endeavors. But how should you behave when you come across an opportunity that seems too good to be true?

Balancing patience with urgency

One day, Suresh was in a supermarket. He was browsing through the aisles to buy groceries. As he was picking up the items, he came across David. David was in flashy clothes and seemed to be wearing an expensive watch as well. They greeted each other as they were old friends and college roommates.

As they caught up with each other, he came to know that David had become extremely wealthy. David was among the first movers in cryptocurrency investments. He had made a lot of money. He then tried to convince his friend Suresh to join him as well. Suresh was hesitant and told him that he too could become as wealthy as him. Suresh declined, saying that he needed to discuss with his wife before jumping into anything. David tried to goad him by making a tasteless joke on his supposed submission to his wife.

But Suresh was unruffled. David then tried to tell him that his company had a limited offer where new members would be given an additional value of cryptocurrency. The time period was to expire that evening. Suresh was tempted, but he held firm and then discussed with his wife. They took a couple of days to discuss. His wife didn't want him to invest in cryptocurrency. As they were discussing, they suddenly heard a news story on the TV that the values of cryptocurrencies had all crashed. Suresh looked at his wife with a sigh of relief.

What: This is a case where Suresh has been given a clear opportunity to make the same wealth as his friend. However, on reflection, he would have also noted that David was among the primary movers.

It stood to the fact that he made enormous profits. But he would not have made the same profits.

Who: Suresh was clear that he needed time to think about investing in such a scheme. He wasn't sure of the technical details, and he did need to discuss with his wife before making any substantial investment into the scheme.

Where and When: Suresh took the right path. Even when he was shown an attractive offer, he knew that he needed the time to think. It is as the adage: *Look before you leap*.

How: As it was a major life decision that would impact the lives of his family, Suresh was right to take his time. He needed the time away from David and his words. He needed to look past his success and examine if he wanted to take such a huge risk in a field he didn't understand.

Why: It can be quite a conundrum when you encounter a situation that demands a quick reaction. A wise person will always take some time to ruminate, reflect and then react. Finding the balance can be tricky as some situations may be temporally bound, and the potential opportunity may not come again.

However, if you think you would be better served if you take your time to reflect and ruminate, then take the time. You should especially adopt a period of reflection when it comes to the issues of finance.

Take your time to mull over matters if the investment would be fruitful. You may also need to budget for any possible emergencies. If many other facets of your life depend on that decision, it would be better to take the time. Major life decisions that could impact a broad scale need reflection and should not be decided on a whim.

After a period of reflection, if you find that your heart and mind agree, then take the relevant action. Some decisions may not need a long period of reflection, while some decisions may need a longer-than-normal amount of time.

Urgency
- Opportunity comes knocking around rarely.
- Some circumstances demand quick reaction.

Patience
- Navigating new directions need knowledge and reflection.
- Sometimes being safe trumps risk when you find yourself in a new avenue.

The key issue here is: While it's okay to take your time, it does not mean that you take too much time. Be quicker in your thought processes. If it involves activities and ideas that you are familiar with, then be quick in your process. Remember, you know what you are doing. Be optimistic about the result.

Being optimistic, as discussed, allows you to get better. However, if it is a new direction and involves new ideas, then don't rush. In such cases, take your time to know what you want and where you could be going. Do not hesitate to explore; ask for guidance and help from others if you need to.

Balance risk vs. innovation:

Even though experimenting and creating something new is thrilling and gives you a high sense of accomplishment, working on a trial-and-error model during tight schedules might not be the best decision. You must understand that taking a risk must not come under the cost of sabotaging a project.

However, do not shy away from risk if the reason is fear. You should know when to be gutsy and when to be conservative.

Points to ponder and reflect upon

- If you find yourself making major life decisions that may include finance, then take your time.
- Understand what you are getting into, especially if it is an area unknown to you.
- Leap only when your heart and mind are in agreement. If even one part of you feels doubtful, then you need time to reflect and evaluate.

As humans are social beings, it is natural to encounter these tensions in our daily lives. The way you resolve conflicts makes a relationship what it is. There is learning in everything if you have the intention to look for it. These are the tensions you cannot run away from. The more you deny a problem, the more significant it becomes. Instead, you must learn to face it and find the balance that can keep you afloat.

PART C: CONCLUSION

5
FINDING YOUR CADENCE
AND THE WIND BENEATH YOUR WINGS

You could see that there are many sets of tensions that you will need to negotiate to maintain your balance in every sphere of your life. I would like to reiterate that there is no perfect midpoint between any of these conflicts. The first step is to identify the problem. Hence, you need to identify the contradictions that may be affecting your balance in life. When you identify the set of contradictions, they need your mediation to find what mix will work for you.

However, as I said in the beginning, finding your balance can be tricky. It takes effort and thought to find it and maintain it gradually. An important aspect is maintaining it on an ongoing basis – which means constant adjustment and readjustment in actions and thought. So, work on these conflicts and contradictions. They will be the making of you. However, I would also like to leave you with a few more important guidelines to help you in this endeavor.

Operate in a band = give yourself some latitude
You are the center of your world= Build a balance around it

When does the pursuit of perfection become a mad quest? How will you know that it is good enough at a certain point?

And, how do you make yourself comfortable with a little imperfection? These are questions worth pondering. Should you be relentless in your quest for perfection? If your answer is yes, you will find that your process will also be severe, and you will be ruthless to yourself. You will be driven by a process that demands the greatest rigor and discipline. It could be from the most basic idea of being punctual stretched to the limit of being a martinet for time. Such self-punishing attitudes can more often be damaging to you. You would constantly demand the utmost from yourself. Learn to give yourself some breathing room and be kind to yourself and those around you.

Learn to be more comfortable with your outcomes and, consequently, your discipline. Allow yourself a marginal relaxation of your guard. Don't be too harsh on yourself when you don't achieve your desired results. In the broader scheme of things, they will balance out when the pendulum swings in your direction.

You grow when you look to balance your contradictions. I would like to reiterate a point that I made in the introductory chapter. Your growth can hardly be achieved through static means.

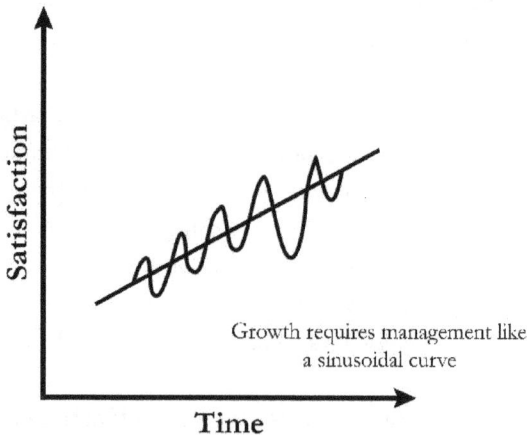

Growth requires management like a sinusoidal curve

Your progression in life will hardly be a straight line across time with increasing satisfaction. It will require the management of your mental energies.

Think of your life in terms of a sinusoidal curve, as shown in the image on the previous page. There will be points in your life when you need to manage your life through the peaks and troughs you experience.

It is important that you keep moving and not get affected by the circumstances. Of course, it is human to be upset about our downfalls; but resilience is something you must practice because life goes on, with or without you. You might as well run along.

You should be aware of your influence on the people around you. Your experience and ability to think and reason will tell you what to take seriously and what to let go of when speaking and engaging with people. Your attitudes and behaviors can impact people for a long time.

As I said earlier, you need to reflect on your journey every once in a while. For example, I'm sure you have heard of the phrase, *Spare the rod, spoil the child*. However, does it mean that you need to punish the child every time they commit a mistake? You need to know what you should take seriously and put your foot down. However, would a softer approach reach your child better than punishment in some cases?

These are the questions you need to ask in any activity that involves parenting and disciplining. Similarly, you cannot be lax and lenient towards your children when they are wrong. There are ways to make them recognize their mistakes without resorting to physical punishments.

Some occasions will need you to be strict, and some you can let it pass. While your role might be to guide your child, you mustn't hover over to the side of living out their lives. This engagement and reflection should not be just limited to your interactions with your children. Examine your engagements with others as well.

Don't be swayed into taking extreme actions due to the heat of the moment. Each of us is unique, so each of you needs to build your own sense of judgment. There is no one-size-fits-all approach. Therefore, develop your own sense of judgment of what you think is right and wrong, and the best strategies to handle things.

You will have your own set of values that will help determine what is right and what is wrong.

However, don't let your thoughts and actions be dictated by what others think and feel. The only way you can balance your life is to do what you believe is correct after considering all the aspects of a situation. Nothing else matters.

Never compromise on your physical health. It is important to have a physical and mental balance to handle the rigors of modern life. Keep yourself physically fit, and you will find that your mind will also be tougher. This requires mental toughness and discipline. So, when you endeavor to make yourself physically fit, your mental toughness and balance will also automatically follow.

Balance between enjoying life and knowing your responsibilities. I'm not saying that you should not make time to enjoy the many pleasures of life. However, remember don't let your pleasures lead you down the wrong path.

For example, when you go to college, you may find yourself suddenly free from the daily surveillance of your parents. This freedom may see you stray down the wrong paths. So, balance your freedom with responsibilities. Always be accountable for your actions. When you start being responsible, you will find that you will develop a natural set of checks and balances to help you avoid straying down the wrong paths.

If you watch professional football, you will hear the top coaches speak of the importance of training. They do value the prodigious talent of the players, but results come from the efforts on the training pitch. They train based on a set of tactics. These tactics require players to follow a set of movements based on where the ball is on the pitch. They also follow a set of consequent reactions based on certain actions.

For example, if a player goes forward to join the attack, someone else will fall in to cover that position. Of course, one cannot account for some unforeseen circumstances.

These circumstances are decided by the talent and skill of the personnel on the field. Likewise, follow a set of tactics for your life.

Follow a routine and set a pattern as much as possible. Building a plan and timeline is critical to be successful.

Following a routine usually helps as it sets a pattern as much as possible. A timetable assists in the predictability of life instead of trying to live life as it comes, which might be okay occasionally. Remember, finding your balance within all the possible tensions comes from practice. So even if you stumble, keep going! One day you will find your right cadence for life, and you will find the same freedom you found in your first unassisted ride.

While you navigate these contradictions and find your balance, it is important to remember that most of these contradictions are based on issues or circumstances you face in your life. You could be brought down by a negative work culture or a soured relationship.

Even when you strive to balance the happiness of others with your own personal goals, these are driven by a need to keep your circle happy. Most of these conflicts arise when we look outward. We are driven by this desire that is often dictated by what could be validated by others. However, when you constantly look outward for fulfillment, you will find that you will never be satisfied and will be stuck continuously negotiating these tensions far more frequently. Hence,

Balance with inner happiness – Do not rely on external factors to make you happy

There is a renowned tale of a farmer. Once a wealthy man was riding on his horse and saw fertile lands lying fallow. This rich man was a merchant of great fame. So, when he saw this land remaining unused, he was enraged. He couldn't understand how a person could let go of such a money-making resource. He rode around and saw a man sleeping on a cot under a tree. He cantered up to the man and woke him up.

He asked him if he was the farmer and owner of the bare land. The farmer acknowledged that the land belonged to him. The rich man couldn't believe it.

He demanded to know why the farmer wasn't growing anything.

The farmer was bemused. He said that he made a good harvest in the previous yield and wasn't in any urgent need of money. The merchant then asked why he would not look to increase his wealth. The farmer then asked him what he would do with increased wealth. The merchant was stumped. He said that he could buy more land to farm. The farmer again asked what he would do with that increased area of land.

The merchant was perplexed. He then thought about it and said with that increased farmland, he could improve his wealth by many folds more. The merchant was flabbergasted when the farmer asked him what he would do with that wealth. The merchant then said he would be able to live in a palatial house. The farmer then asked again as to what he would be able to do with a stately house.

The merchant then waxed lyrical of the many luxuries he could enjoy, including a bed in a room with a roof. The farmer then asked again what he would do with these luxuries. The merchant was ticked off. He said that he could be happy. The farmer then smiled and said that he was already happy. Why should he put in such efforts just to end up back in the same state?

There has to be a point in your life that you have to reflect on your pursuit. How much is enough? How much of your mental and emotional well-being will you compromise in the quest for external pleasures? External factors, usually material/related signals, are fleeting. They are brief because they have an impact on your life as long as you let them. Constantly ask yourself if you will be really happy chasing a certain goal. Contentment requires constant reflection. You can only find it when you look for it. When you constantly reflect on your pursuit to find balance, you will find inner peace. I understand that it can be tough to switch to this mentality as every accomplishment that is lauded and celebrated are external accomplishments. You would have been introduced to the top scorer in your class or school as the model student in your childhood. This would never stop, as a new peak will show itself when you reach the summit of a challenge.

This endless quest is the trapping of chasing external goals for happiness. External factors can occasionally make you happy. But real happiness comes from within you. With a well-balanced life, you strive towards internal happiness.

Internal happiness stems when your bearings are well balanced in your mind. It comes from within the core of your being. When you are at peace with yourself, you will find that there are only a few or no unanswered questions.

You will find that you would have justified or rationalized and made peace with most questions. And crucially, you will find that you are happy about the outcome. When it comes to finding your inner balance, others' thoughts mustn't sway you. As I mentioned before, you need to provide the worth for yourself.

If you look outward, you will find that you are constantly pulled in different directions. When you are looking for inner peace, you must become the captain of your own ship. Don't let others garb your life. One of the crucial ways to ensure that you drive your life is to run your life at your own pace. Internal happiness stands the test of time and situations.

No matter where you find yourself in life, a well-balanced life will ensure your happiness. You will know how to negotiate your contradictions and choices and make the apt decision. Your internal happiness will be reflected in your confidence in dealing with and managing those situations.

Pacing your life - Building the right balance of pace

Run your life at your pace. Don't be overwhelmed by the pace of your peers. Find the cadence that gets you the best balance and speed. Just as you cycle through the back-alleys or the busy traffic-laden road, you will find the right speed to navigate these roads.

You will know when to weave in and out to avoid the potholes and negotiate the speed bumps without falling. Similarly, find your own pace. There are many stages you will find yourself in as an individual.

When you start your career, you will find yourself alone; soon, you will be married, and later you could also find yourself as a parent. You could go through many phases until it is your phase of retirement. Every step comes with its own set of challenges and accomplishments and many various changes. There will be parts of your career and life that will demand you to put your head down and slog it through. It will demand the utmost from you – especially your college years and the initial years of your job or profession.

These phases can find their echoes in Hinduism, where we speak of the four stages of life: Brahmacharya (student), Grihastha (householder), Vanaprastha (forest walker/forest dweller), and Sannyasa (renunciation).

So, cycle through these phases at a pace that you find comfortable. As you find your rhythm, you should remind yourself that there are some absolutes in life. Even when you cycle the road, you are expected to follow the traffic rules. You cannot break them, and there is no compromise on that account. Likewise, in life, there are some absolutes that you cannot cross. You have to follow the law of the land and stick true to your values and ethics. When you start to set the terms for your own life, you will make one important discovery.

You will find that your contradictions will be fewer and much easier to negotiate. You will find that the balance in your life would be much easier to find. If you cast your mind back to your early efforts in learning cycling, you will find that most of your problems stemmed from your mind.

There would have been occasions when you had a prolonged stretch of riding unassisted. However, there could have been a sudden thought. A sudden fear of falling may have struck you. This fear would have caused you to immediately stop, or you would have found yourself falling.

That fall was not caused by any lack of technical skill. It was a fear produced in your mind, and it affected you. But when you learned to ride freely, there would be no more lingering thoughts of failure plaguing your mind.

All Balance is in the Mind

The easiest way to avoid complications in your life is to stick to your integrity. Integrity is that honest voice inside of you. Listen to it and let it reflect in your thoughts and actions. When you listen to your inner voice and practice it in your daily life, you will find that even the trickiest choices become easy to negotiate. When you are honest with yourself, you will find it easier to reconcile with your choices and decisions. When you can reconcile with your choices and decisions, you will find that balance isn't far away. Hence,

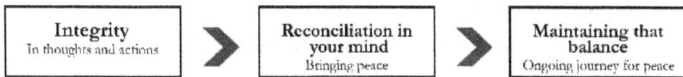

Integrity In thoughts and actions	**>**	Reconciliation in your mind Bringing peace	**>**	Maintaining that balance Ongoing journey for peace

Swami Vivekananda said it best when he said that we should be like the lotus in the pond. When the lotus flower thrives in the pond, the water does not stick to the flower.

And like Debbie Ford said, *"Like the lotus flower that is born out of mud, we must honor the darkest parts of ourselves and the most painful of our life's experiences, because they are what allow us to birth our most beautiful self."*

We need to rise out of the murky depths and bloom. We do that when we are a part of things but have a sense of detachment. We should maintain our independence, character and integrity. You need to be true to yourself. If you deviate from what gives you balance, your life will be subjected to a phase of turbulence. When you don't maintain your balance on your cycle, you will fall. Likewise, you will be dissatisfied and grumpy when you stray away from the pillars that give you balance.

You will feel that you are not fulfilling your potential. Thus, make sure you are constantly maintaining the balance. When you have pockets of time in which you have just rested/ taken it easy, then balance it with periods of intense work.

Keep your balance, mentally and emotionally.

Simplify your life. Because once you simplify it, you will know what you care about the most. And then you stand for that. But how do you simplify it? To achieve serenity in your mind, you need to accept the consequences of your choice and move ahead by knowing that you made the right decision.

This is what gives you a balanced state of mind. There will be situations where you will find yourself at an intersection of two pathways, one that you know is the right way to go and another that contradicts it. The latter might present itself with many perks, even if they are momentary. But if you are not honest with yourself, you will complicate your life.

Nothing that is built on the foundation of lies has lasted very long. So, you must learn to stick with your integrity. Resolving a conflict with your own self is harder than resolving a conflict with others. However, try to avoid conflicts with others because conflicts happen when there are overlaps. When you minimize your footprints, you minimize conflict.

"In whatever you do for a particular person, a city, or a state, assume the same attitude towards it as you have towards your children - expect nothing in return." – Swami Vivekananda

In this book, the contradictions mentioned are the ones that I have seen or observed in many. But one of the subtexts I am leaving out of all this discussion is the ability to train the mind to be open to diverse views on the spectrums. That is also a key transferable skill that would be helpful to many nuanced situations that you will likely come across. As you read all this content about balancing your life - you realize the external forces playing on you constantly. You need to balance against all these to avoid getting toppled over. To work through these counter-balancing forces, keep yourself at the front and center. Always do things that you believe are correct after weighing them over from all aspects of a situation. Also, in some sense, you are narrowing and zooming back to your core and center.

118

If you do that, and I do not mean it in a selfish sense, then your balancing becomes that much easier. Because your heart will tell you and calibrate for you if you are going overboard with any reaction. It also shows you the importance of "going back to basics."

Remember: You are in charge of your life. No one else is. You are what you make yourself to be. So, struggle against all the conflicts to find your balance and soar into the skies.

ABOUT THE AUTHOR

Srihari Palangala is a thriving leader and the Marketing Director for Dell Technologies, responsible for marketing strategy and execution of the Mid-Market segment in the Asia Pacific/Japan, EMEA and China regions. He has previously held roles as the Director and Head of Marketing for Dell Technologies in India and the Head of Marketing in the APJ region, Dell Technologies. He has spent two decades working with technology products in various roles, including business development, consulting and marketing across the United States, India, Asia Pacific and EMEA.

Srihari is the recipient of the "India's Greatest CMO 2016-17" by - AsiaOne's India's Greatest Brands & Leaders 2017 and "Leading CMO of the Year 2017" by The Enterprise IT Leadership Awards. Srihari is also recognized at Dell World-Wide as among the top 'Marketing Inspiring Leaders' in the organization in 2018 and the "FY '19 APJ Marketing Outstanding Leader of the Year" award. Srihari is a graduate of the Indian School of Business (ISB) and also holds a Masters in Computer Science from Arizona State University.

Srihari holds a great interest in teaching and coaching. In his career, he has taught students from high school to the postgraduate level in many reputed B-schools. From his teaching and mentoring experiences, Srihari has learned and experienced the importance of balancing the many contradictions life throws at him. Srihari continues to hold an active interest in business, marketing and personal / team development to engage with students and corporates alike.

He can be reached at his LinkedIn Profile - https://in.linkedin.com/in/sriharipalangala. Alternatively, you can also scan this QR code:

www.ingramcontent.com/pod-product-compliance
Lightning Source LLC
Chambersburg PA
CBHW031515040426
42445CB00009B/246